In Search of
Atticus Finch
A MOTIVATIONAL BOOK FOR
LAWYERS

Mike Papantonio

A SEVILLE SQUARE BOOK
Pensacola, Florida

SECOND EDITION

A SEVILLE SQUARE BOOK
SECOND EDITION

Seville Publishing
Correspondence:
>Post Office Box 12308
>Pensacola, FL 32581
Offices:
>316 South Baylen
>Fourth Floor
>Pensacola, FL 32501

IN SEARCH OF ATTICUS FINCH
—A MOTIVATIONAL BOOK FOR LAWYERS
First Seville Square Edition, January 1996
Second Edition, September 1997
>Editorial assistance and book design: R. B. Shackelford
>Cover Design: Cynthia Turner

ISBN 0-9649711-1-9
Seville Square Books may be obtained for educational, seminar, or promotional use in bulk quantities at discount rates. For information, please write to:
Promotional Department, Seville Publishing,
Post Office Box 12042, Pensacola, Florida 32590-2047

Also by Mike Papantonio

*Clarence Darrow the Journeyman
—lessons for the modern lawyer*

ACKNOWLEDGMENTS

KEN BAILEY
DIANA BAILEY
BILL BAKER
SUZANNE BARNHILL
SONNY BREWER
VIRGINIA BUCHANAN
DENNIS FITCH
NICK GEEKER
CHARLES GIBSON
ROSS GOODMAN
BEN GORDON
ROBERT GORDON
JAMES HALEY
ROBERT HEATH
RICK KUYKENDALL
MARTIN LEVIN
JOHN MERTING
JOHN MORGAN
LARRY MORRIS
JACKIE RION

FOREWORD
by Morris Dees

Robert E. Lee Cope was a man at peace with himself. His province was Bullock County, Alabama, and his world revolved around the courthouse in Union Springs. He was my lawyer, handling real estate transactions when I purchased farm land adjacent to my home county of Montgomery.

Lawyer Cope was a real-life Atticus Finch. He knew everybody in town, and they knew him. He never got rich, but had the love, confidence, and respect of most everyone. When I visited his office, he took time to discuss philosophy, politics, civil rights, and the latest plays he and his wife had seen on their annual visits to New York or to the restored Springer Theater in Columbus, Georgia.

Bob Cope was a wonderful father and a devoted husband. He gave the poor a voice in court, often without payment, and he stood against the powerful when justice was in the balance. I often said that the Bob Copes were the real winners in our profession.

You can also be a winner, as a lawyer, a parent, a spouse, and a person. And you can do it in the context of our fast-paced modern legal system. You can start by searching for Atticus Finch.

Mike Papantonio has written a wonderful book that should be required reading for every law school freshman, and then required rereading for lawyers five years into practice. I found Atticus a few years before Mike graduated from high school. Atticus helped change my life. I graduated from law school in 1960 and, within three years, I had over a hundred open files, had lost my sense of humor, and was seeking another way to make a living. I had dreamed of being a lawyer during those hot days picking cotton on my father's small farm, helping people win justice and making myself a good living, but

I was not pleased with what law practice was doing to me as a person.

On a warm June night in 1966, I saw *To Kill A Mockingbird* at a local drive-in theater. The Civil Rights Movement was happening all around me, and I was sitting it out. When Atticus Finch walked out of the empty court-room after the jury ruled against his client and the upper gallery, stilled packed with black folks, rose in his honor, tears were streaming down my face. Why couldn't I be a lawyer like Mr. Finch?

A year or so later, I was fortunate to read Clarence Darrow's autobiography, *The Story of My Life*. Darrow and Finch were cut from the same cloth. I decided to take control of my life and begin to be human again.

Over the years, I have tried big cases from coast to coast, been the subject of a television movie, written two books, appeared on dozens of talk shows, and built the Southern Poverty Law Center. But I hope I have never lost touch with being real to my clients, opponents, friends, and family. I try to look at the world and myself as Darrow or Finch might.

We cannot turn back the hands of time to when small-town lawyers dealt with small-town issues. We cannot ignore high-tech computers or laser disc evidence presentations (I am typing this on my 1955 Smith-Corona Manual because I like the feel of words being put on paper), but we can keep in mind that we are representing real people with real problems against opponents who deserve civility and respect.

Take a few hours from your busy practice and read Mike Papantonio's thoughtful and useful book. He is a highly successful lawyer who has taken time to share some valuable lessons. You'll be a better person for the effort.

Rolling Hills Ranch
Mathews, Alabama

INTRODUCTION

In 1960, J. B. Lippincott Company published a book by a young Alabama woman that became an instant best-seller and critical success. It went on to win the Pulitzer Prize in 1961 and was later made into an Academy Award winning film.

Today, with over 15 million copies in print and translated into ten languages, the book is regarded as a masterpiece of American literature. The movie has become a film classic.

The young woman was Harper Lee, of Monroeville, Alabama; her book, *To Kill A Mockingbird.*

In addition to being a story of extraordinary power and universal appeal—Warner Books' latest cover proclaims Ms. Lee's book a "timeless classic of growing up and the human dignity that unites us all"—*To Kill A Mockingbird* has special lessons for those of us who are lawyers.

It is hard to imagine anyone who has not read the book or seen the movie in which Gregory Peck so powerfully portrays Atticus Finch. Finch is a small-town lawyer appointed to defend Tom Robinson, a black man accused of raping a white woman. His noble effort sets off a crisis of conscience that rocks the sleepy but fictional Southern town of Maycomb, Alabama.

For those who have read or viewed *To Kill A Mockingbird*, I ask you to do so again, for Atticus Finch represents what I believe to be the best of what being a lawyer is all about. If we understand Atticus, we will better understand ourselves. As we get further from the essence of who we were or set out to be when becoming lawyers, many of us find ourselves unsatisfied and unfulfilled.

Put another way: In a time when so many of us are full, maybe even filled with all of life's financial and worldly blessings, yet still unful-filled, Atticus Finch, a full-service lawyer provides an example any trial lawyer might well emulate.

As an epigram for her book, Harper Lee chose this line:

> *Lawyers, I suppose, were children once.*
> Charles Lamb

Significantly, I believe, Atticus is seen through the eyes of a child, his young daughter, Jean Louise Finch, affectionately known as "Scout."

Scout and her older brother, Jem (Jeremy Atticus Finch), are learning the lessons of life, growing up, and observing the behavior of adults and the community. But most of all, they are being taught by the example of Atticus Finch a tremendously complex yet simple character possessing almost every quality a human being and a trial lawyer might wish to have. In a clear and definable way, Atticus Finch epitomizes "quality" in most all his functions, both public and private.

Or, as another character, Miss Maudie, says to Scout, "Atticus Finch is the same in his house as he is on the public streets."

That is, as a private person—father, family man, friend, neighbor—he is the same man he is in public as a lawyer, legislator, and citizen of his community. He brought the best qualities he could muster to all of his many roles.

As we come to know him better, we also will come to know ourselves better, and, I believe, solve many of the problems we as trial lawyers say we have.

That said, let me point out that *In Search of Atticus Finch: A Motivational Book for Lawyers* is a road map.

The road begins where we are.

It leads to where many of us say we want to go.

We intend to find Atticus Finch in ourselves and go home richer for the journey.

Why is this search worthwhile?

Because Atticus was a decent man who chose to be a lawyer. He was not worried, stressed, or burned out by practicing law. He knew who he was and what he was up to. He was motivated, purposeful, and of service to himself, his family, and his community. Depression times had made him poor, but one has the feeling that being rich would not have changed him. He had more time than we have, for Harper Lee tells us a day in Maycomb, Alabama, in the 1930s seemed like it had more than 24 hours in it. Atticus had time to be noble and thoughtful and to live a full and meaningful life.

Any full, meaningful life has problems, and his did. His neighbors had problems: one was a reclusive loon; another was old, crotchety, and dying; many were blindly prejudiced; some were enlightened but unable to do what was right.

Atticus's clients had problems: Tom Robinson was fighting for his life; Walter Cunningham was concerned about maintaining his pride, keeping his land, and figuring out how to pay for legal services in a time when there was little or no money in circulation. Atticus's children had the ultimate problem of growing up. But Atticus's problems did not define him. He was defined by his beliefs, values, and lifestyle. He found and implemented solutions, or, when necessary, accepted that no just, fair, and noble solution is fully possible, but that one does one's level best to live life honorably and decently anyway, without recriminations or regret.

Despite being at the heart of a great controversy and being on the unpopular side of an emotional and irrational issue that ripped his town apart, Atticus was steadfastly true to himself. Even while losing the biggest case of his career, he ultimately retained the respect of his family, his friends, and the community whose higher and best interests he *served*.

In a time when we know for an absolute fact that our fellow citizens do not see lawyers as serving but rather as self-serving, it is clear that we need to do several things, among which are:

- Realize or actualize a higher and better self-image.

- Learn how to live both our law practices and personal lives in a more Atticus-like way.

- Over time, convey to others this truer image of who we are and what we do to *serve* our fellow citizens.

I hope this "search" for Atticus Finch will help all of us reach that desired higher ground.

One final word: I am a trial lawyer, a plaintiff's lawyer. It is what I practice, what I do. Naturally, this book is written from that perspective, but I believe the lessons Atticus Finch has to teach will prove valuable to all who practice law.

> ***J. Michael Papantonio, Esq.***
> Pensacola, Florida
> Fall 1995

CHAPTER ONE

HOW I DISCOVERED ATTICUS FINCH

I am not certain when it first became apparent to me that being a trial lawyer brought with it certain unique versions of stress or posed a greater potential for "burnout" than most professions.

After my first 10 years of practicing law, it was easy to recognize that the price we pay to be the best we can be in our profession is sometimes steep. Moreover, from conversations over the years with my colleagues in the legal profession, I discovered both implicit and explicit evidence that we all had made trade-offs in achieving professional success. Most have few regrets about those trade-offs, but many in the process of lawyering recognize that sometimes this price is too high.

I believe we can do a great deal to make our lives as lawyers both more meaningful and more productive by addressing personal and professional issues in a more Atticus Finch–like way.

My discovery of that simple fact came by a rather circular route. Despite being located in the far reaches of northwest Florida's outback, I am often invited to speak at legal seminars throughout the Southeast on such topics as cross-examination, product liability, or the use of demonstrative evidence. My awareness of a lawyer's unique problems addressed in this book began in 1993, when I was asked to speak to a gathering of Mississippi Trial Lawyers on the subject of "Staying Motivated as a Trial Lawyer."

I felt I was wearing out my old speeches anyway, so I was delighted to produce some new material. I began at libraries and bookstores, certain that in the 200 years of trial lawyers, one or more of us had addressed this subject, and all I would need to do was add to what others had said.

What I found was the opposite. There were motivational books and articles for insurance executives, insurance adjusters, and insurance salesmen; motivational and leadership books for corporate executives; inspirational books for health care providers. Almost every group we initiate lawsuits against has tapes, videos, and books telling them how to stay happy, healthy, and prosperous in their stressful corner of the world.

But I found nothing for lawyers.

After going to libraries and bookstores, I called the ATLA and ABA thinking that surely they had reams of material profiling issues that concern trial lawyers. I found data from questionnaires; profiles; information from studies exploring personality traits, characteristics of trial lawyers . . . 200 years' worth of history of trial lawyers; but the only meaningful documentation was a report called "At the Breaking Point—The Emerging Crisis in the Quality of Lawyers' Health and Lives, 1991." This document, I can assure you, was anything but motivating. Any lawyer reviewing it would feel compelled to run out immediately for counseling as a result of all the gloom and doom between the lines of that report.

In addition to that report, I found a jewel of a book written by what must have been one of the most unhappy attorneys ever to hang out her shingle. Her book was devoted to explaining to other lawyers why they should get another job, how they could go about getting another job, and how happy they would be once they were no longer practicing attorneys. The title of the book was *Running from the Law: Why Good Lawyers Are Getting Out of the Legal Profession.* It was filled with captivating chapter titles such as "Assuming a New Identity," "Making a Break," and "Recommended Career Alternatives."

It was a dismal assessment of our level of happiness and/or dissatisfaction with what we do for a living.

Although I was not that unhappy and most of my colleagues did not seem to be so disgruntled, I nevertheless thought I should accumulate some meaningful information profiling what we are about as trial lawyers. A reasonable survey seemed like a proper way to go, so I set out to ask a representative sampling of lawyers about the state of our profession.

To arrive at some understanding of what kinds of questions such a document should contain, I conducted interviews with dozens of attorneys who were willing to discuss their concerns, their worries, and their personal rather than statistical satisfactions and dissatisfactions as trial lawyers.

After sifting through topics that surfaced consistently in these interviews and discussions, I created a set of 25 multiple-part questions with multiple-choice answers. I then mailed them to more than 200 trial lawyers throughout the Southeast.

WHAT YOU TOLD ME

The response rate was an astounding 90 percent. The complete Survey and Results are contained in the Appendix of this book, but I want now to talk about what I later came to regard as the single most important question asked and answered.

With a single exception, the highest percentage response received was from the 76.2 percent who said, *"I need to take more time from my day-to-day practice to improve my quality of life."*

The top dissatisfactions listed are as follows:

> 57.5% – *I have become less of a legal scholar and more of a businessman.*

> 56.3% – *The quality of life I have with my family suffers.*

> 40.0% – *My emphasis on making money detracts from my creative, inventive ability as a lawyer.*

36.3% – *I have always wanted to forge new fields and concepts in the practice of law, but I do not have the time.*

31.3% – *The public image of plaintiff's trial lawyers affects my self-image.*

Below are responses to the question, "Which of the following do you notice about yourself now that you did not notice when you first began practicing as a trial lawyer?"

48.6% – *I am much more suspicious of everyone.*

41.1% – *I cannot relax.*

38.6% – *I find I have more of a negative outlook on life in general.*

These responses were contrasted with only 17.4 percent who were able to say:

I have never been happier.

I have become more creative and well-rounded in my personal life.

Among the responses to, "List the most significant fears you have about your practice as a trial lawyer," were

> 64.1% – *Fear of spending too much time practicing law and not enough time living.*

> 49.9% – *Fear of burnout.*

Things were worse than I had suspected. This was not so surprising, though, when it registered with me that, in truth, many of us simply have not paid attention to the fact that practicing law sometimes requires inappropriate and unnecessary sacrifices. Among them is the willingness to make our own profession our absolute, number-one priority.

In most cases, it seems never to have occurred to us that we were entitled to and could have the higher quality of life the survey indicated so many of us desired—or that we could live full, meaningful lives and practice law at the same time.

It was then that I thought of Atticus Finch.

REMEMBERING ATTICUS FINCH

I had read *To Kill A Mockingbird* for the first time many years ago as a high school student, and I had read it a second time as a college student. I had hoped I might become a lawyer very much like Atticus.

I respected his character as a good neighbor, a scholar, a family man, and an honorable attorney as much as I respected his tenacity as an advocate for a just cause.

What I remembered most about Atticus Finch was that he was a truly decent human being who had simply chosen to practice law in the same way he lived his life: honorably, with sensitivity, care, and intellectual honesty. His level of self-awareness enabled him to be far more aware of and sensitive to the feelings and needs of others than most of us are. He was, indeed, the same man on the public streets that he was at home, but there was far more to him than that.

His life, like ours, was divided into the normal functions of being both a public and private person. The public man in him was a lawyer, legislator, and citizen of his community. As a private man, he was a father, family man, friend, neighbor, teacher, and scholar.

In all of these difficult and complex roles, Atticus acted with real quality. His relationships had quality, and his professionalism as a lawyer and citizen was exemplary. Whatever he touched, win or lose (and he did lose the biggest case of his career), was elevated slightly. Every man, woman, or child who had contact with Atticus was better for it. It was as if in being noble he ennobled all who came in contact with him.

Moreover, I saw a great contrast between the way Atticus was regarded in his community and the way lawyers are regarded today. We live in a time when "lawyer bashing" seems to be the national pastime.

Although a great number of his fellow townsfolk frown or downright viciously convey their disapproval of Atticus's defending a black man accused of raping a white woman, almost no one loses respect for him. In fact, many appear to respect him even more when the case is over. He is due respect because of the way he lives his life.

Atticus, however, is "bashed" for undertaking an unpopular cause. He can refuse to take the case, but he does not. Some of his fellow citizens say he is *going against his own kind* by defending Tom Robinson, an innocent and honorable black man, against rape charges made by Bob Ewell, the lowest form of life in Maycomb County.

But, no one, not even his detractors, bashes Atticus for being a dishonorable man. Many of his neighbors believe he is wrong. Even his friends believe he is naive and blind, but not dishonorable as a man or as an attorney. His children are bashed at school because Atticus is defending a "Negro." When his daughter, Scout, defends him by beating up an antagonist in the schoolyard, Atticus explains to her his situation and hers in this way:

"Scout, you aren't old enough to understand some things yet, but there's been some high talk around town to the effect that I shouldn't do much about defending this man..."

But he goes on to say that if he does not give Tom Robinson his fullest and best representation, he cannot hold up his head in town, cannot represent Maycomb County in the legislature, cannot even ask Scout and Jem to mind him. It is clear that for Atticus to ask others to do their duty, to do what is right, and expect them to do so, he also has to do his duty to himself and others. "Scout," he says, "simply by the nature of the work, every lawyer gets at least one case in his lifetime that affects him personally. This one's mine, I guess."

Scout asks,

"Atticus, are we going to win it?"

and Atticus says,

"No, Honey. . . . [but] simply because we were licked a hundred years before we started is no reason for us not to try to win."

Today, when winning seems to be everything, I wonder if such sentiments might not be regarded as absurd, however sincerely spoken.

Yet in our survey, some 48 percent also said, "I have or will have made a meaningful impact to better society as a whole by the time I leave my practice as a trial lawyer," and 51.1 percent agreed with the statement, "I am a trial lawyer because I enjoy conflict *when I am on the right side.*" [emphasis added]

In *To Kill A Mockingbird,* Atticus Finch clearly does have a meaningful impact in bettering society, even though he fights in a losing cause. When his son Jem suggests to Atticus that the jury has failed miserably in Tom Robinson's trial, Atticus points out,

"No, it didn't," he said. "That was one thing that made me think, well, this may be a beginning. That jury took a few hours. An inevitable verdict, maybe, but it usually takes 'em just a few minutes..."

Atticus is right when he says it is "a beginning." In ensuing decades, the struggle for equal rights and new legislation, as well as for a new understanding among people, has made juries far more colorblind than when he lived and practiced. Point is: Lawyers like Atticus Finch have had "a meaningful impact to better society."

The question I wanted to ask, and honestly answer, was, *inasmuch as I started out to be a lawyer much like Atticus, have I succeeded?*

My answer was, "Only partially," which led to the next question: "Why not fully?"

HOW IS MY LIFE DIFFERENT FROM HIS?

I tried to define the differences between Atticus and most of us. The most obvious differences were these:

He lived in a small town.

Most of us live in big cities.

He lived during the Great Depression.

We live in an age of affluence.

On the whole, he had the respect of his community because his fellow citizens truly knew him as a whole person, not just as a lawyer.

On the whole, simply because we are lawyers, we do not inspire such respect, regardless of our overall qualities as human beings.

He had time for his family throughout his entire life.

Most of us have convinced ourselves that we will someday have time for our families, but not right now.

Atticus's office in the old Maycomb County courthouse "contained little more than a hat rack, a spittoon, a checkerboard, and an unsullied Code of Alabama."

Our offices are the tallest and the grandest. They are beehives of activity. We are computerized—in instant communication with our fellow lawyers within and without the firm, and with the world at large. Our law libraries are five times the size of Atticus's whole office. We are "surfing the 'Net."

At first glance, it seems as if we have everything at our fingertips while he had nearly nothing. Yet a deeper look tells us that he was a far more learned man than most of us. The book tells us that he never went to "school." Nevertheless, he was still evolving intellectually and spiritually at the age of 50. Most of us stopped evolving after 19 years of school.

Furthermore, in the movie *To Kill A Mockingbird* old Judge Taylor walks down the street, sits with Atticus on the front porch, and asks him to take Tom Robinson's case. The judge knows that Atticus will take the job and what an awful burden it is to do so. Atticus and Judge Taylor respect and trust each other. Their personal knowledge of each other allows such respect to develop.

Most judges before whom many of us try cases are strangers to us socially and professionally. They have as much reason to doubt us as we do them.

The differences go on:

People communicated with Atticus and he with them, face-to-face, citizen to citizen, neighbor to neighbor.

We communicate by fax, phone, and letter and only rarely in person, face-to-face.

Atticus walked back and forth between work and home four times a day.

Many of us are often two connecting flights away. "At work" can mean anywhere in the United States for days and weeks at a time.

"Overdoing it" and overachievement were suspicious conduct in Maycomb County. Atticus's world recognized both as illnesses.

Overworking, "overdoing it," and overachievement are admirable traits valued and promoted by our clients, partners, and peers.

In Atticus's world, things meant what they meant, people were what they were and seldom changed. For better or worse, people were true to themselves and who they were, and what they stood for was clear and definable.

We live in a world where almost nothing means what it purports to mean; it is all imagery, bits and bytes. People may or may not be true to themselves, but either way, we have no real means of saying who is who and what is what.

From what you, my colleagues and peers, tell me in survey and personally in conversations and interviews, almost all of us are in the same boat.

IS ATTICUS THE RIGHT MODEL?

After considering all the differences, I began to wonder whether Atticus Finch is a model for the last decade of the twentieth century. In contrast to Atticus's slow-burning life, our survey showed that 68.2 percent of us believe we are Type A personalities. We all know generally what that is, but more specifically, Type A behavior is:

A special, well-defined pattern marked by a compelling sense of time urgency — "hurry sickness"—aggressiveness and competitiveness, usually combined with a marked amount of free-floating hostility. Type A's engage in a chronic, continuous struggle against circumstances, against others, against themselves. The behavior pattern is common among hard-driving and successful businessmen and executives— but it is just as likely to be found in factory workers, accountants, even housewives. About half of all American males—and a growing number of females—are more or less confirmed Type A's.*

---

*From the cover blurb of Drs. Meyer Friedman and Ray Rosenman's famed book *Type A Behavior and Your Heart,* (Alfred A. Knopf, 1974), wherein they show that "more than 90% of the people having heart attacks prior to the age of 70 are Type A's."

It does not get much more in "in your face" than the above, and a little over two-thirds of us say Type A behavior describes us.

Not only is Atticus not in anyone's face, but when Bob Ewell confronts him on the public street after Tom Robinson's trial and spits in Atticus's face, Atticus—calmly restrained anger and distaste clearly written on his face—takes out a handkerchief, wipes off the spittle, but refuses to sink to a lower level, saying later that he only wished Bob Ewell didn't chew tobacco.

If Atticus had practiced law among the legions of Type A personalities that make up the world of modern trial practice, wouldn't he have been trampled underfoot?

My inclination by this time was to ask, "What has Atticus Finch—a small-town lawyer in a bygone time—got to do with me?"

Yet, on reflection, the answer was still, "Everything!" Certainly, we have impediments that Atticus did not have when it came to enjoying the kind of full and meaningful quality of life that he did. But it became clear to me that if we dealt with those impediments in the same way Atticus dealt with his life, many of them would disappear, and many of our problems would be more easily and satisfactorily solved.

For one thing, Atticus's power is found in his restraint. The "in your face" approach to trial practice that has been evolving since the early '70s would no doubt have been an annoyance to him, but the contentious, combative trial lawyer of the '90s would be easy pickings for brother Finch. Atticus leads, Atticus teaches, and Atticus persuades with his force of character and intellect. What a mismatch!

More and more, I came to see that Atticus Finch is fully equipped, indeed, to compete with the best trial lawyers we could field today. In fact, and for all I was able to tell, Atticus might have been a Type A personality living a Type B life by sheer force of will.

If so, many of us who are Type A's might aspire to do likewise, for in so doing, Atticus creates and controls the quality of his life and the lives of those with whom he comes in contact. More and more, I came to understand there was much to learn about this small-town trial lawyer and the way he lived.

The vast majority of us say we wish to have a better quality of life. We define that as spending more time living and less time immersed in the practice of law. We all have impediments that Atticus did not worry about. Some of these are mentioned above, and others will be cited in subsequent chapters. Most of these problems and impediments can be handled by exploring the way at least one great, fictional trial lawyer lived.

In our responses to the survey, we say we want to live less stressful lives where the threat of "burnout" does not hang over our heads. By searching for Atticus Finch all of us might find ourselves on the right track.

"Stress" and "burnout" are not issues in *To Kill A Mockingbird.* Atticus Finch is not "stressed out." If he has any fear of "burnout," Harper Lee does not mention it.

Chapter Two

ATTICUS FINCH DOESN'T LIVE HERE ANYMORE— WHY NOT?

The world in general and the world of courts and law specifically have become something quite different from what they were in Atticus's time, and we all know it. Obviously, then, we should discuss how a person like Atticus would meet the world's new challenges.

Human nature has not changed one whit since Joshua fought at Jericho. We meet today the same problems Atticus faced a few decades ago.

The problems are dressed differently and travel at a higher speed, but they are the same nonetheless.

Yet, as indicated by both my survey and a dual survey (1984 and 1990) by the Young Lawyers Section of the ABA, modern-day trial lawyers have or claim to have a number of specific problems that Atticus Finch clearly did not have. I believe the main ones we should address here are:

Inordinately high levels of stress and fear of burnout

High levels of dissatisfaction with the profession as it exists today

Lack of gender equality in the practice of law

Atticus Was Not Stressed or Burned Out

I said in Chapter One that "stress" and "burnout" do not appear in *To Kill A Mockingbird*. That omission ought to tell us something.

Almost 50 percent of those responding to the survey say one of the most significant fears we have about practicing trial law is "fear of burnout." Some 42.5 percent said that the level of stress experienced by trial lawyers is "more than moderate," and 15.7% said we experience "extreme stress." Therefore, 58.2 percent reported that they are experiencing more than moderate to extreme stress.

There is a clear, well-understood, and documented relationship between stress and burnout, and Type A behavior. By definition, Type A behavior is "hurry sickness." It may be that "hurry sickness" is "stress" itself.

Harper Lee describes the town of Maycomb, Alabama, as "a tired old town" where, in Atticus Finch's time, "people moved slowly . . . a day was twenty-four hours long but seemed longer. There was no hurry. . ."

Atticus had one courthouse to attend. We, however, in some cases, have a dozen to appear in, and on some days, we are scheduled to be in all of them at once.

Atticus had time to live. We are short of time to the point that our capacity for overdoing has dulled our capacity to take a breath, much less live. But we do, in fact, live in and deal with a Type A world, a hurry-up workplace that a great many studies seem to indicate spills into our personal lives so that we are trampling ourselves to death even to "have fun" or "recreate." Even our futile attempts at self-renewal with "quickie" cruises or "long weekend" vacations often leave us more fatigued than before we left.

We even have invented a new vocabulary to describe this place and time in which we live—*stressed out, bummed out, burned out.* We all know the words. We are perfectionists, doers, and overachievers. We practice "gamesmanship." We are "looking out for number one." We are "masters of one-upmanship."

The Japanese use a catchy little word to describe the twentieth-century compulsion of overworked attorneys. They call it *hatarakisugi,* which, loosely translated, means to overwork the mind, the body, and the spirit until one dies from exhaustion.

Atticus Finch does not have any of those words to describe himself or the world in which he lives. The question might be whether we need them? Many of us have grown to believe that this new vernacular describes a way of life successful attorneys must simply endure. It may be that when we believe in such words or concepts we actually create or validate them, trapping ourselves in their webs.

For example, when the people of Salem, Massachusetts, believed in witches, they found and burned them by the dozen yet have not found a half-dozen since they stopped believing in such things. Is it possible that when we start believing in a more rational life, we will find it?

What is the solution to resolving or overcoming all these differences between where we live and where Atticus lives? Since we cannot significantly change or slow down the world, only one thing can be changed: ourselves.

Anyone who thinks Atticus Finch was not under pressure in both his public and personal lives is not paying attention. As we know, human nature has not changed much since the beginning of recorded history. What has been ever-changing, even in recent decades, is *human behavior.* For example, *pressure* does not cause Atticus to exhibit "aggressiveness and competitiveness . . . combined with a marked amount of free-floating hostility." It did not cause him to be "stressed out" or to be fearful of "burnout." It makes *us* all of these things.

The pressure to hurry apparently plays a larger role than we would like to admit in causing us to do all of the above. A great many of us are already predisposed to or infected with Type A "hurry sickness." In addition to that predisposition, we attempt to throw fuel on the fire by the way we practice law. Many books say too much of this kind of "good thing" can kill a person.

Despite this obvious fact of a trial lawyer's existence, we know better; we wish to do better; we long for at least a fair portion of another kind of existence, a more Atticus-like life. The survey indicates that the great majority of us are of mixed mind and divided feelings about what we do. For example, some 64.8 percent surveyed said, "I am a trial lawyer because I like the excitement and fast pace," but nearly the same number (64.1 percent) say our greatest fear is "spending too much time practicing law and not enough time living."

That seeming contradiction says that we are torn between a deep desire for slowing down long enough to "smell the roses" and a compulsion to drive Formula One race cars ever faster in circles until we crash.

Let me ask you this: At 150 miles an hour, can you hang your head out the window and smell anything but hot asphalt and the exhaust fumes of the car ahead of you? And from what many indicated, the smell of the exhaust ahead of you makes you want to overtake whoever is up front. Then that old competitive, aggressive, barely concealed free-floating hostility begins pumping.

Indeed, everything in our experience constantly reinforces this desire for instant everything. We require more and more speed and productivity

—more and more of everything. At the same time, we give ourselves no time whatsoever to enjoy the kind of life that such productivity and accomplishments can provide.

Underlying these compulsions are powerful parts of human nature—ego and desire for material things. Atticus does not burden himself with that type of weight because he does not define his success or value as a person by his level of acceptance or by his material worth. He is able to slow his life down because he understands what is of eternal value in his life. It is his sense of service, his grace, and his unflappable decency that give his life value and allow him to slow down and live!

We say we want more time "for living" and, moreover, want to improve our quality of life, but our drive to succeed, our Type A personalities and behaviors, simply will not let us take the big foot off the accelerator and slow down.

We see this dichotomy because we are rational people. In fact, that ability basically defines what a trial lawyer should be: a rational, analytical, problem-solving professional. One veteran battle-scarred attorney explained it to me this way: "I have kept my horse at full gallop from battlefield to battlefield, trial to trial, judging my worth only by my victories."

Unlike many of us, Atticus is not of a mixed mind, but rather of a firm, well-grounded one. He simply does not allow himself to be measured and defined by how much he produces or accomplishes on a particular day.

Atticus does not play the hurry-up game nor, I suspect, would the game be playing him. It plays many of us as if we were violins. No matter what, if he lived today, here and now, no matter how fast the world around him went, Atticus Finch would be unflappable, both as a lawyer and as a private person. He would control the rate at which his world traveled and his heart beat.

One key to that characteristic seems to be that Atticus knows himself, knows who he is, where he is, and what he is up to, what he is about. He is living a balanced life. Many of us have lost our sense of balance. Some few have even become unhinged.

Observing others is easy work for lawyers. For that reason I believe Atticus Finch can be of service to us. If we understand him, his life, his way of handling things, and his method of meeting life's challenges, we can develop a habit of asking ourselves, "What would Atticus Finch do and how would he do it?"

The point is that he has what between two thirds and three-fourths of those of us who are trial lawyers say we want according to our survey.

Before we can take concrete steps to solve the mystery of why we, of all people, do not have what we want in the measure we want it, we have to do what we do best: We have to analyze where we are and where Atticus is.

Only after we have done our homework and understood ourselves and Atticus Finch better can we discuss a number of specific ideas that might help us adapt or adjust our personal and professional lives toward a more Atticus-like posture.

Is Atticus Dissatisfied, Unfulfilled?

I do not think so. If he is, Harper Lee, in writing *To Kill A Mockingbird,* says very little about it.

On the other hand, and to varying degrees, many of us say we are both dissatisfied and unfulfilled as lawyers in the '90s.

Results from the *National Survey of Career Satisfaction/Dissatisfaction,* Waves I and II, conducted by the ABA Young Lawyers Division in 1984 and 1990 shed some light on these topics.

In 1984, the first study, Wave I, established a baseline as to who in the legal profession was satisfied and who was not. It also determined what areas of dissatisfaction bothered lawyers who were generally satisfied with their practices. The 1991 follow-up, Wave II, resurveyed as many previous respondents as possible, and also surveyed a new sample.

The bottom line was that the level of dissatisfaction was significant.

Among those lawyers in private practice who planned to change or had changed jobs, 40 percent gave as their reason, "I want more time for myself and my family."

These figures do not prove anything, but they indicate that a great many lawyers want the same things my survey says trial lawyers desire, neither of which Atticus Finch had to "want."

First, Atticus's life is balanced between being a public and a private person—having professional duties and a family life; second, Atticus is driven by a desire more for excellence than for financial improvement. Everything that Atticus does implies that his excellence will triumph and he will succeed because of the way he is motivated. One has the feeling in reading *To Kill A Mockingbird* that the only thing keeping Atticus Finch financially "poor" is the Depression, which kept almost everyone poor. He certainly is not poor in any other way.

Regardless, the ABA's study indicates we may be going in the wrong direction for achieving either excellence or personal satisfaction. We are, the study says, suffering from "time famine" and "time deprivation." Of the 20 percent of lawyers who say they are, for whatever reason, entitled to five or more weeks of vacation, only 8 percent actually took the time. Of the 26 percent who are allowed four weeks, only 16 percent took even that much time. Exactly half the lawyers reporting in 1990 worked between 200 and 239 hours a month.

Atticus does not suffer from "time deprivation" or "time famine," as we do. Even as hours worked have gone up, the demands each of those hours has placed on us have also increased, or, according to the ABA survey:

> The pressures and demands of law firms and clients, *the element of speed* [emphasis added] created by the advent of fax machines and computers, and the increasing lack of courtesy between lawyers—to name just a few of the factors that create strain between lawyers—have together changed the quality of the hours worked so that 200 hours in

today's practice is far more stressful than 200 hours in the 1960s.

Only 33 percent of the lawyers surveyed were "very satisfied" with their job setting. Nearly half, 48 percent, fell into the "somewhat satisfied" group. I am not sure that being "somewhat satisfied" with what I do would suit me well enough or be what I'd call a plus toward acquiring a higher quality of life.

I suppose the worst news is how people deal with the stress of lawyering. Coping with the stress of lawyering resulted in the following for our tightly wound group:

> 79% — *Get anxious*
> 39% — *Eat more*
> 37% — *Become depressed*
> 52% — *Become more critical of myself*

Are we having fun yet?

Among possible practices that are considered good practices for dealing with stress, the following percentages of lawyers do not do them.

65% — *Do not exercise*

60% — *Do not talk with close friends or family about stress levels*

88% — *Do not practice meditation or relaxation exercises*

59% — *Do not look at things humorously*

Even with these inordinately high numbers of attorneys who stated that they were stressed and dissatisfied because of their jobs, less than 10 percent of those questioned in my survey said they had ever read a motivational or self-help book of any kind.

For centuries, great thinkers, philosophers, and sociologists have been writing, teaching, and preaching about the various methods for fixing one's spirit when dissatisfied and stressed. Some of those ageless cures will be discussed in this book.

For now, let me just point out that Harper Lee created Atticus as a lawyer who, during the course of her story, carries the weight of the world on his shoulders in Alabama's Maycomb County in the 1930s. Moreover, he is a single parent raising two children as best he knows how during the worst economic times in American history.

The legal fight he finds himself undertaking in the small community of Maycomb County is one that he knows he has lost from the start. The repercussions of that unwinnable fight place him and the two people he loves most in serious jeopardy, both emotionally and physically.

Yet even within *that setting,* Harper Lee creates a character who understands and teaches his family to understand the simple song of the mockingbird. As we analyze Atticus, it is my hope that we hear that song more clearly.

A Great Woman Created Atticus as a Model for Lawyers of Either Gender

In 1990, the American Bar Association conducted a study showing that 22 percent of the male respondents placed themselves in what the ABA categorized as a "high strain" group. By contrast, this study showed that a higher percentage (44 percent) of the female respondents placed themselves in a "high strain" classification. An interesting article entitled "Myths vs. Ms.: Why Women Leave The Law," appeared in the Winter 1986 issue of *Barrister* magazine. That article suggests that women are more dissatisfied in their jobs than their male counterparts because their tension level as lawyers is high and they have very little time to themselves in their private lives. The article also suggests that the overall atmosphere in this predominantly male-dominated profession is foreboding at best.

My purpose here is not to argue gender bias, which I believe exists, to the detriment of our profession. Instead, I believe it is more important to analyze whether or not Atticus's formula for living works well for women in our profession.

Harper Lee was a prophet in that she understood more about the art of successful lawyering and living for both women and men thirty years ago than most of us as practitioners understand today. The character she created in Atticus Finch is as close to a *Shaolin* master as any legal hero in American literature.

The *Shaolin* warrior/monks developed and mastered the art of defense without weaponry or armor.

Similarly, Atticus protects himself with armor that does not weigh him down. He masters the use of powerful weapons that are hardly visible to his opponents. He is not combative, contentious, aggressive, or overtly warlike in any way.

In fact, his children describe him as feeble, since he is nearly fifty years old. His son complains that Atticus is too old to be tackled while playing touch football, and he is nearly blind in one eye. He is not interested in hunting, fishing, or playing poker. Scout describes her father this way:

> Our father didn't do anything. He worked in an office . . . he didn't

drive a dump truck . . . he was not the sheriff . . . he did not farm, work in a garage or do anything that could possibly arouse the admiration of anyone.

His children constantly question his manliness. He plays checkers, he plays the Jew's harp, and, according to his children, he mostly sits around the living room and reads. There exists absolutely no apparent testosterone-drenched machismo in the character of Atticus Finch.

However, it would be impossible to analyze Harper Lee's creation and not recognize the power and forcefulness of his character. The genius of Harper Lee is that she has created the ultimate warrior who, at first glance, carries no weapons.

Rather, the power of Atticus Finch is found in his high level of self-awareness and self-acceptance. He is not the sheriff, a truck driver, or a garage mechanic. He is not the athletic football player that his son wishes he could be. Atticus is aware of those realities, and he accepts them.

Along with an extremely high level of self-awareness and self-acceptance, Atticus accepts almost everyone for who he or she is and tries to deal with them within those confines.

When Atticus is faced with taming Scout's combative tendency to fist-fight her way out of most problems, he tells her this: "You never really understand a person until you consider things from his point of view . . . until you climb into his skin and walk around in it." Atticus recognizes that dealing with most people in a combative, confrontational way is counterproductive. The "in-your-face" or "Rambo" approach to dealing with people and problems is a style of lawyering that would be foreign to Atticus Finch, or, as Scout says:

> I have heard that lawyers' children, on seeing their parents in court in the heat of argument, get the wrong idea: they think opposing counsel to be the personal enemies of their parents, they suffer agonies, and are surprised to see them often go out arm-in-arm with their tormenters

during the first recess. This was not true of Jem and me. We acquired no traumas from watching our father win or lose. I am sorry that I cannot provide any drama in this respect; if I did, it would not be true. We could tell, however, when debate became more acrimonious than professional, but this was from watching lawyers other than our father. I never heard Atticus raise his voice in my life, except to a deaf witness.

Atticus does not require testosterone and machismo for facing down lynch mobs or confronting hostile witnesses. He deals with lawyering problems the same way he deals with family problems—with intellect and compassion.

We all know there are times in any trial or situation where a certain forcefulness, even harshness, is necessary, perhaps appropriate, but those times should be rare.

Atticus and Miss Maudie Are Reflections of Each Other

In Atticus's time, "this year of grace, 1935," in Maycomb, Alabama, women did not practice law. But in *To Kill A Mockingbird,* many of the clear insights into who and what Atticus is come through his neighbor and good friend Miss Maudie Atkinson.

It is Miss Maudie who tells Scout that, "Atticus Finch is the same in his home as on the public streets," and it is she who sees and explicates those things of which women perhaps do have a more intuitive grasp. Miss Maudie says to Scout:

> "You are too young to understand it . . . but sometimes the Bible in the hand of one man is worse than a whiskey bottle in the hand of—oh, of your father . . . if Atticus drank until he was drunk he wouldn't be as mean as some men are at their best. There are just some men who—who're so busy worrying

who—who're so busy worrying about the next world they've never learned to live in this one, and you can look down the street and see the results."

Through Miss Maudie's insights, we learn that Atticus is a balanced human being and lawyer—not soft but rather possessing a manliness that also embodies its own finer side. In the literature of self-help and enhanced personal relationships today, it would be said that Atticus, a man in all senses of the word, embraces and allows his humanity and gentler side to be expressed.

The ABA's studies and the article cited earlier seem to be saying that women who are trying to be more manly in the practice of law are not finding acceptance. For example, a year after the previously cited article, "Myths vs. Ms.: Why Women Leave The Law," appeared in *Barrister,* another article entitled "Frustration of Women Lawyers" appeared in *Trial* magazine. It suggested that many of the skills and attitudes required to be a successful trial lawyer are skills and attitudes that are not well accepted in women. The article suggested that the female lawyer who excels with lawyering skills considered admirable in a male attorney, is considered "aberrational and unattractive." The article goes on to suggest that women are, therefore, condemned to engage in the battle of lawyering *without armor.*

Yet, in fact, *that describes Atticus Finch at law.* What I am suggesting is that Atticus's basic values and demeanor in life and law practice are just as appropriate for women, who can be feminine yet forceful, more successful, and happier with themselves and the practice of law.

The truth is that the practice of law needs less machismo on the part of lawyers of either gender, and more grace, humility and decency in the way lawyers interact with each other and the rest of the world.

Some attorneys I have talked with, both male and female, have suggested that it may be more difficult for women to emulate Atticus Finch, as many women lawyers, between home and career, may have far more roles to play than most men. I think Atticus shows that we all have many roles to play and that those roles should not be conflicting within the context of being good lawyers as well as excellent human beings.

Atticus Finch is a single parent who plays the role of mother and father to his children. Of course, he succeeds only with the help of his sister and his neighbor, Miss Maudie, and the good services of Calpurnia, the family cook, and perhaps because he is seldom far from home. Maycomb is a small town.

The real point is that those qualities of self-awareness that enable Atticus to be more sensitive or aware of others really are in some measure those qualities many writers of this generation speak of as making for a fuller and more caring human being, man or woman. The magic of Atticus Finch is neither male nor female. It is human, and all lawyers can benefit from becoming more human. However you cut it, being Atticus-like is not a gender question.

Chapter Three

ATTICUS SERVED HIMSELF, HIS FAMILY,
AND HIS COMMUNITY—DO WE?

More than we sometimes give ourselves credit for, those of us who are lawyers do serve our communities and the nation as a whole. I think it is significant that some 48 percent of questionnaire respondents stated that a primary reason they were lawyers was that they hoped to have made a meaningful impact in this world by the time they leave their practice.

This response is a direct measure of a desire to be of "service," as well as a statement of faith that large numbers of us not only believe we want to serve but that we have served or will succeed in serving. Too bad almost no one in America appears to know it but us.

As I said in opening this book, we know for an absolute fact that our fellow citizens do not see us as serving. They see us as almost exclusively self-serving.

Does this skewed public image that we are learning to live with have any impact on our self-image? Some 31.3 percent of our respondents say yes, it does.

Pre- and post-survey interviews indicate to me that some of us in answering that question may have been too proud to admit we are so thin-skinned that this public perception affects us.

We have to face the facts. Our skins are not as thick as we would like to believe. It seems to be difficult for us to find happiness about who we are when friends, family, and neighbors believe everything they read about us in the papers. Instead of being portrayed as mostly decent men and women practicing law and living by acceptable rules of conduct and social responsibility, we have lately witnessed our profession under aggressive attack by all of the media. For example, we've seen,

> Weak-chinned, sniveling lawyers being gobbled up by Jurassic dinosaurs as moviegoers applauded wildly.

> Prime-time TV advertisements where sweaty obese lawyers have been chased down and roped like cattle in an ad agency's attempt to sell Miller Lite Beer.

I cannot imagine a movie or commercial where Gregory Peck as Atticus Finch would be portrayed in such a way. The problem with our public image (and, many say, self-image as well) is totally related to whatever differential there is between how well and truly we serve our communities and how they believe we serve or fail to serve.

Rob Gordon, an attorney with the New York firm of Weitz & Luxenberg put our problem in perspective this way:

> The customer is always right. Either we have failed to be of service, or we have failed to let anyone know about our service. I think it is the latter. Whichever it is, we have a problem with how people perceive who we are and whether we serve.

Atticus Finch does not have that problem. He knows he is serving the highest and best interests of his "society," however small Maycomb County may be. He knows he serves. They know he serves.

Despite standing up for what is an unpopular cause to many of his less enlightened fellow white citizens, Atticus serves them just as surely as he serves Tom Robinson during the ugliest trial in Finch's career. The citizens of Maycomb cannot put their finger on exactly how Atticus serves them by fighting so hard for the life of

Tom Robinson, but their respect for Atticus suggests they ultimately understand.

There is a strong powerful scene, one you will want to read more than once, that shows Atticus at his best.

Suspecting a lynch mob may try to come for Tom Robinson at the Maycomb County Jail, Atticus leaves home in mid-evening. He is next found by his children propped back in a chair at the jail door, facing down a crowd of men. You would think he would have a gun, but he has only his trusty newspaper.

Things go from bad to worse when Atticus's children and Dill show up, endangering themselves, but Atticus does not back down.

He is saved by Scout's reminding Walter Cunningham, one of the mob leaders, who Atticus is, what Atticus means to him as well as to all of Maycomb.

Walter Cunningham eventually says to the mob, "Let's clear out," and they do. The threat over, Atticus tells Tom Robinson to get some sleep, then picks up his chair to leave.

As Atticus picks up his chair, even the small boy, Dill, suddenly understands just who Atticus is and how important he is because of what he stands for.

> "Can I carry it for you, Mr. Finch?"
> asked Dill. He had not said a word
> the whole time.

Acquiescing, Atticus says graciously,

> "Why, thank you, son."

The tribute and respect Atticus receives for a lifetime of service as both a lawyer and a human being run even deeper, wider, broader than we first realize. They cross lines of age, gender, and even race in a time and place where race is the deepest and most cruel division of all.

Although, in the middle of the Depression, Maycomb County, Alabama, blacks do not vote or wield political power, their full respect for Atticus is shown in one of the most powerful and moving scenes in the book.

It occurs just after Atticus has fought hard to win an acquittal for Tom Robinson, but has failed. in reality what has happened is that the jury has failed, the system has broken down, and justice has not been done. We are all familiar with such travesties.

Scout and Jem have been sitting in the high balcony with the blacks, next to Reverend Sykes, Tom Robinson's pastor.

Judge Taylor polls the jury. Scout relates the following:

> I peeked at Jem. His hands were white from gripping the balcony rail, and his shoulders jerked as if each "guilty" was a separate stab between them.

Atticus shoves his papers into his briefcase, speaks briefly with the court reporter and the prosecutor. He whispers something to Tom

Robinson, pulls on his coat and leaves, walking down the middle aisle. Scout says:

> I followed the top of his head as he made his way to the door. He did not look up.
>
> Someone was punching me, but I was reluctant to take my eyes from the people below us and from the image of Atticus' lonely walk down the aisle.
>
> "Miss Jean Louise?"
>
> I looked around. They were standing. All around us and in the balcony on the opposite wall, the Negroes were getting to their feet. Reverend Sykes's voice was as distant as Judge Taylor's:
>
> "Miss Jean Louise, stand up. Your father's passin'."

Has any trial lawyer ever had a simpler but more

extraordinary tribute? Are there any among us who would not trade several million-dollar verdicts for such an expression of appreciation and admiration.

WHY DOES IT WORK FOR ATTICUS AND NOT US?

We recognize that most of us serve our clients and our community as honorably and decently as Atticus. We would like to believe that people recognize our service; most of the time they do not. What did Atticus do that we are failing to do in getting that message out?

Atticus Finch, the individual, the lawyer, both as a public and private man follows a very basic simple formula for creating the public image he is blessed with in Maycomb, Alabama, circa 1930. Sixty years later, this formula is still relevant for each of us no matter where we live. The formula has a universal appeal and relevance.

Atticus's answer, his secret, is that most of what he does is not self-serving. He always makes it his goal to give more than he gets in return.

Secret? I do not think so.

Even your old granny could have told you that chickens come home to roost. The concept that the good we do in the lives of others is returned in our own is an ancient one. Atticus believes it and applies it in his life. Such an idea seems foolish to the misanthrope but seems academic to Atticus. Atticus sows rewards everywhere he goes. Ultimately both Atticus and everyone who comes into contact with him reap good from his actions.

Take it from Atticus's life itself. The morning after he has lost the most critical case of his career and has gone to bed "not bitter" but "tired," he awakens and finds the family cook, Calpurnia, setting a plate of chicken on his breakfast table. If that is not symbolism for a chicken coming home to roost, what would be?

Calpurnia says, "Tom Robinson's daddy sent you along this chicken this morning. I fixed it."

It goes on and on: food has been heaped upon his doorstoop the morning after the trial, and what does *To Kill A Mockingbird* say about how Atticus responds?

> Atticus' eyes filled with tears. He did not speak for a moment. "Tell them I'm very grateful," he said. "Tell them—tell them they must never do this again. Times are too hard." He left the kitchen, went into the dining room and excused himself to Aunt Alexandra, put on his hat and went to town.

We might ask ourselves what kind of public man appears that morning on the streets of Maycomb, Alabama?

Is he faced with a public image crisis?

Dill's Aunt Rachel's reaction to Atticus's representation of Tom Robinson is: "If a man like Atticus Finch wants to butt his head against a stone wall, it is his head." What does her remark mean? Not that he's a bad lawyer and damned fool but that a man of Atticus's character and integrity is entitled to do as he pleases. He is free to do what he believes is right because no one on his earth—his small plot of Maycomb County—expects him to do otherwise. He is expected to give more than he takes.

What do our clients and communities expect of us? If not the same reasoned and justified integrity and character Atticus exhibits, we need to do something about it.

This lesson is one of the most significant in this book because to me it is the lesson Atticus Finch's example teaches. It is a lesson we will also find taught overtly in well over half the motivational or self-help books ever written and implied somewhere in the rest. It is an elixir touted as a cure for everything from anxiety to depression, or whatever ills these books purport to cure.

For example, in his *How to Stop Worrying and Start Living,* Dale Carnegie gives concrete advice on how to deal with almost all of the gremlins that trial lawyers face in their practice from stress and worry to achieving a higher quality of life. Carnegie says that he conducted his life by applying the following rules:

> The simple act of thinking each day of how you can do something— just one thing for someone else— will cure all sorts of problems in your life.

> If you forget about yourself and do something for others each day to improve their lives, the quality of your life will improve.

Nonsense? No doubt it must appear that way for the average Type A lawyer of the '90s, but the simple truth is that these rules work. If most of us were to analyze closely when we are truly the happiest, it would probably be during the times that we have served others.

Chickens really do come home to roost. They do for Atticus, a lawyer in the '30s, and they will for lawyers in the '90s. Some concepts are timeless.

IF NO ONE KNOWS WE ARE ATTICUS FINCHES—WHY NOT?

Another moderately disturbing facet of our being trial lawyers and having a bad image surfaced in my survey. To the statement "Some older, successful, trial lawyers have caused much harm to the image of trial lawyers through the excessively boastful image they have portrayed to the general public," the respondents answered:

> 44.8% – *Yes.*
> 24.1% – *No.*
> 31.0% – *The good they have done outweighs whatever harm they might have caused.*

I think we need to take to heart the message this breakdown sends. If almost 45 percent of questionnaire respondents say excessive boatfulness has caused harm and only 31 percent say the good outweighs the damage, we have acquired a real problem we didn't need. Jackie Rion of Charleston, South Carolina, observed:

During the '70s and '80s, every trial lawyer who received a verdict for more than a million dollars had to rush to the media and talk about how his or her verdict was the biggest in the country. The lawyer of the '70s and '80s wanted to talk about his multimillion-dollar verdict in terms of what a talented lawyer he was instead of addressing the important issue of how deserving his client was. He wanted to emphasize his savvy rather than publicize the service he had performed for a deserving client.

Another theory that is extremely pervasive among lawyers analyzing the demise of the trial lawyer's public image centers on the publicity explosion the legal field has witnessed within the last ten years.

According to an overwhelming majority of attorneys interviewed, huge Yellow Pages ads, billboards, and bad-taste advertising have denigrated the public image of lawyers everywhere.

It has been argued that in any given hour in any city in America, the public sees our profession selling itself cheaply to anyone and everyone who has experienced personal tragedy or misfortune. Money for nothing is what the public hears in thirty-second sound bites.

In most law offices, almost no portion of the advertising budget is devoted to explaining how attorneys serve the community. Instead, there is a fixation on boasting about how successful and clever we are in the courtroom.

I think my point is clear. We might at least be Atticus-like enough to blow someone else's horn rather than our own. If a jury returns a massive verdict for damages, the award still is for those damages, not for our performance. The message should be that "we served."

If we have improved someone else's life with our talent, if we have served, then that message will surface without our cheapening the story. A natural order of living that is as basic as the physical truth is that for every action, there is an equal and opposite reaction. Perhaps Harper

Lee understood physics more completely than most trial lawyers.

How Can Service Remedy the Situation?

Larry Morris, a Florida trial lawyer who has been practicing law for more than fifteen years explained that his need to serve is so fundamental that he equates it with his need to learn and his need to compete.

> I never set out to reap rewards or be recognized when I am in the process of truly helping someone improve their life. There are, however, very few times that I can recall when my efforts to help have gone unnoticed or unrewarded.

There is no doubt that on the whole lawyers serve clients and communities. We can, however, do better. We can also improve our way of communicating our service to others. Atticus's mere presence on the public streets and in his home among family, friends, and neighbors, is adequate to convey who he is and what he does. Personal contact is a good way for us to convey ourselves to a great many people. But, because the wider community in which we live and work is so vast, so distant, and so unable to see us fully, I believe we must design ways and means of conveying a truer image of ourselves.

And I do not mean by some sound or news bite that is just more slick media hype. I am talking now about the sincere and modest conveyance of the good we do for others – our clients, our communities, our cities, states, and nation. When we truly serve without expectations of rewards and recognition for that service, those around us will notice that service.

ATTICUS SERVED HIMSELF AND HIS FAMILY

I believe we do serve our communities. However, many of us do not believe such service reflects upon us personally or on our families nearly as well as it should. We suspect that our job of serving others does not always benefit those closest to us.

Fifty-six percent of us say a major dissatisfaction of trial lawyers is that our job causes the quality of life we have with our families to suffer; 64.1 percent say our greatest fear about our practices as trial lawyers is "spending too much time practicing law and not enough time living."

This response is unfortunate. Any lawyer with significant expertise and experience and sufficient years in practice to have built a good reputation usually earns a good living. We seem to be starving in the midst of a cornfield or vegetable patch. If we agree that what we do (and are) has not yet served all the facets of *our* lives, where does that leave us?

CHAPTER FOUR

IF WHAT WE DO AND ARE IS NOT SERVING ALL THE FACETS OF OUR LIVES, WHY NOT?

When I began to think of Atticus Finch as the model lawyer and human being, it was because everything he did in his practice and in life seemed to work at a more effective level than the way our surveys indicate our own nonfictional lives do.

We could explain quite simply by saying that Harper Lee had the advantage of writing Atticus as she wanted him to be, a man in harmony with himself and attuned to the lives of others even when beset with external conflicts and immersed in normal problems.

We have all heard that there are three kinds of people: those who make things happen, those to whom things happen, and those who wonder what happened. As trial lawyers, we generally do our best to make things happen on behalf of our clients, but apparently, we fail to do the same for ourselves. When it comes to clients, we pry and shovel their problems here and there. Push comes to shove in trial, and most of us would like to think that we give better than we get in that arena.

Where the surveys indicate we fall short is in the area of working too much and "living" too little, and at times in failing to manage time in such a way as to have some left for ourselves and our families. A statistically disproportionate majority of us suffer from an inability to regulate our expenditure of personal energy so that we have enough for both our practice and our lives.

As one of the most rational problem-solving

groups of professionals on earth, it is obvious that once we recognize and define our problems, we generally are rather effective in solving them. I would like to think that we could write a script for our lives as artfully as Harper Lee wrote the script for Atticus Finch. If we were writing such a script, we certainly would not be inclined to create a character who has a fear of burnout as one of his most significant fears as a trial lawyer.

Nevertheless, almost 50 percent of questionnaire respondents stated that they have a fear of burnout. I believe the reason is fairly simple: The unregulated, irrational expenditure of personal energy is an inefficient and often ineffective way to live. As every human being has only so much energy to give, so much to burn, it is obvious that burning too much results in "burnout."

To some extent, our job description invites us to distribute our allotted energy to everyone except ourselves.

By choice and profession, we enter into agreements every day to use our energy for solving conflicts for our clients. By way of agreement and, in fact, *duty*, we allow our clients to visit their stress, anxiety, frustration, worry, and conflicts, on our lives. We bear that burden because it is part of our job description and because we owe it to our clients to do so.

Their fights become our fights, their wars our wars. We take their causes seriously; we take these obligations to heart. We also are highly competitive, and once having taken up a cause, we strive mightily and even single-mindedly to prevail on a client's behalf.

We choose to do this. Some 64.8 percent say, "I am a trial lawyer because I like the excitement and fast pace"; 54 percent explain that, "I am a trial lawyer because this is what my personality is best suited for."

Although being a lawyer is what we have chosen and what we say we are suited for, we also recognize that this choice inherently contains a number of undesirable aspects. Stress, worry, anxiety, fear, anger, and conflict are not things easily left at the office at the end of the day.

Another undesirable aspect of our "choice" is that each of these negatives burns up a huge amount of our energy.

Two questions you might ask yourself are:

> If what I do burns up or consumes more energy than I can personally afford—why?

> In what way can I either acquire more energy or practice law less?

One possible answer may be the simplest. *Acquire more energy.* We can do so by saving energy that we now waste.

The easiest way is to look at useless energy burners and eliminate or mitigate them. Literally hundreds of books and articles written on this topic hypothesize that stress, anger, anxiety, fear, worry, and conflict are all useless energy consumers.

ATTICUS IS A SLOW BURNER

All these facets of the same emotion are, experts say, characterized by patterns of behavior that Atticus Finch does not engage in. In fact, my observations of Harper Lee's character lead me to conclude the following:

> Atticus expects a lot from himself in the way he conducts his life, but he does not visit those high expectations on others. In fact, he expects of others only what he knows they can do, not what he wishes they could do or believes they should do. I think that attitude provides a huge energy savings for Atticus.

> If the conduct of others truly does affect Atticus seriously enough, he attempts to influence that conduct by teaching through word and deed. He finds peace for himself when he understands his role as a peacemaker rather than an antagonist.

He handles or deals with stressful
or worrisome events in a calm
and judicious way. His response
to most things in his practice and
his life is measured. He places
limits on the amount of energy
he is willing to expend unnecessarily.

These attributes are indicators of a kind of
rocklike self-assurance. We have hints of how
he has acquired it. Harper Lee tells us he is self-
educated, well-read, broad, and deep in his
assimilation of life experiences and learning.
What he has learned has helped him avoid the
rapid burn of energy fueled by visceral emotion.

ATTICUS DOES NOT LET THE CONDUCT OF OTHERS INFRINGE UPON HIS PERSONAL BELIEFS

Experts appear to agree that people who suffer
from stress and anger do so primarily because
they feel infringed upon or frustrated, or because they attribute intentional wrongness to

the behavior of others. We have all had these feelings, at every level from the important to the trivial.

For example, one judge before whom you often appear constantly rules against you on motions, on procedural issues, and on evidentiary issues. You are irked because in your heart you suspect this judge has a political agenda. You believe he has quit being a judge and is acting as an advocate for the other side.

You suspect he rules against you intentionally to embarrass you, to frustrate you, to attack your beliefs and convictions as a lawyer. You think you should be able to expect more from this judge, but your client and you are being victimized by this judge's intentional wrongness. Some of what we believe about what people are doing to us has some basis in truth.

However, much of what we believe most of the time has very little basis in reality. We just feel that things are wrong, out of kilter, and we feel that surely they are that way by intention, that whatever has struck us as wrong is deliberate and aimed at us. We assume we are being persecuted when doing so is completely inappropriate. All of that unnecessarily burns energy. We do so often; Atticus does so seldom, if ever.

Atticus seems to know exactly where to draw the line between his own beliefs and practices and those of others. He seems to know that what he does is right for him and most probably right for others—if they are seeing clearly.

But his expectations of others are never based totally on his own terms. It is not that he is nonjudgmental; rather, he measures the lives and actions of others by what they can do instead of what he would have them do.

Instead of attributing intentional wrongness to the bad behavior and beliefs of others, he knows that many of these people—his neighbors, his fellow citizens—are simply ignorant of higher values and incapable of clearer beliefs *at a particular time.*

He does not seem to give up on them. Rather, he administers a gentle poke here, a slight shove there, a word here, an example there—he teaches. He recognizes that they are subject to coming around at any time, always aware of the fact that he may be the one who is not seeing clearly. The bad thinking of others simply cannot infringe upon his own clear understanding.

He does not take other's actions personally. It is plain that in every situation, in every encounter, in every conflict, Atticus recognizes and understands (or tries his very best to understand) what others are doing and why. Then in a calm and rational way, he takes whatever action he believes will help them come to a higher or better understanding. He attempts to lead them to higher ground.

Although he is somewhat frustrated by wrong-mindedness, he refuses to buy into the kind of frustration that for most of us is a counterproductive energy burner. Far more than he at first appears, Atticus is a man of action. He is not a person who goes around wishing things were different. He does not let the fact that he cannot make things totally different, totally right, totally good, totally perfect, in one fell swoop, keep him from doing what he must do now! He would appeal the wrong decisions of the judge described above. He might even work to have him unseated as a judge. That done, he would not waste one whit of energy in worrying about what he cannot do, or in frustration over what others cannot do or have not done.

He would not allow someone else's wrongness to borrow or steal his valuable energy. In fact, Atticus might even recognize that there is a natural order in life that holds someone like a wrongheaded judge accountable for his wrongness. Atticus does not allow stress, worry, anxiety, anger, or conflict to burn an inordinate amount of energy.

The principle is important. I only wish I had been smart enough to make it up, for it goes right to the heart of avoiding what we call stress —a true bugaboo for the 52.8 percent of us who experience it at "more than moderate" to "extreme" levels. I suspect that the 37.1 percent who said they experience "moderate" levels of stress also may be measuring what is moderate by the modern experience. That is, we fully expect a day filled with conflicts and flaps, problems, deadlines, and commitments.

From more subjective data, interviews, and conversations, I believe many of us have come to view certain relatively high levels of stress as "normal," even "moderate." Only 4.5 percent say they experience "mild" levels of stress.

As Atticus appears to experience only mild levels of what we today call "stress," we might say far too few of us travel the public streets as calmly as he does without stress or go home to the peace he enjoys. One reason he does so and many of us do not is that he simply and rationally does not let other people erode his firm beliefs and create frustration and anger.

He does not entertain any foolish assumptions about what others intend. He operates on the assumption that almost every human being—with very few exceptions—is doing the best possible with what he or she has. Even when his fellow townsmen are doing things he knows are not good, not fair, not right, he does not attribute wrongful or malicious intention—what we might call bad heart— to their actions.

He does not demand that the world run as well as he wishes it would. For example, he explains to his children that Mr. Cunningham, who leads a lynch mob after Tom Robinson, "just has his blind spots." Atticus recognizes that Mr. Cunningham simply is not equipped with the intellect to appreciate the wrongness of his action.

However, Atticus is unwilling to burn up energy on the type of anger, anxiety, or stress that people like Mr. Cunningham sometimes create in many of us. Mr. Cunninghams are epidemic in most of our practices.

This clearer, deeper view—this broader understanding—apparently reduces Atticus's level of stress greatly, leaving a lot of energy that otherwise would have been wasted for him to apply to more effective living. We might wish to consider his method and do likewise. The way we can do that is simple. We should pay attention to what we are doing and how we are thinking. We are too rational a group to keep repeating what we know is useless. Atticus sees traps; he avoids them. Surely if we see them, we will avoid them, too. His is a way of thinking that most of us would do well to adopt.

HOW ELSE DOES ATTICUS AVOID ENERGY–BURNING TRAPS?

It is extremely important to understand that the character created by Harper Lee is a character who accepts who he is and his place in Maycomb, Alabama. It does not appear that he is ever looking too far down the road to see whom he is going to pass, and he is never looking over his shoulder to see who is getting ready to pass him.

Atticus is bold in his honesty with himself and about himself. For example, a simple dialogue between Atticus and Scout illustrates his self-acceptance and self-approval. Scout asks Atticus why people pay for his legal work with such things as produce and firewood, and Atticus explains that everyone is suffering hard times in the Depression. He says people do not have any money. Knowing he does not have much either, Scout asks: "Are we poor, Atticus?" Atticus says, "We are indeed, Scout."

That exchange does not suggest that Atticus is complacent in his desire to do better for himself and his children. He is just unwilling to burn energy worrying about the fact, that on that day in 1935, during a conversation with his daughter, life is difficult financially. His acceptance of that fact in no way interferes with his desire or ability to do better. He makes himself comfortable with the space he occupies at that particular moment. Perhaps he instinctively recognizes that stress is generated and unnecessary energy is expended by constantly placing oneself in the process of being someone that one is not—yet!

My number-one pick in the long list of attorney stressors and energy burners is our unwillingness to approve of and accept where we are in our careers, *today*. It's as if we were blind or, as the late Walker Percy put it in *Lost In The Cosmos: The Last Self-Help Book:*

A stranger approaching you in the street in a second's glance sees you, will size you up and place you in a way that you cannot, and never will even though you have spent a lifetime with yourself ... why is it that in your entire lifetime, you will never be able to size yourself up as you can size up somebody else?

One young attorney analyzes himself this way:

I waste an awful lot of my resources expecting too much from myself at this early stage in my career. I am Bob Jones, not Morris Dees. I have been practicing 10 years, not 25. I handle auto cases, not complex high-profile civil and criminal cases. I eliminate a lot of stress when I remind myself of those things.

Attorneys who seem to experience huge amounts of stress are the ones who are unrealistic about where they really are on their career path. Why were they not being interviewed by CNN about the big case? Why were they not obtaining incredible results in trial? Why were they not speakers in state and national seminars? They lose sight of where they are and where they should be.

Almost without exception, this "I am behind" attitude surfaced in interviews with lawyers who have practiced less than 10 years. A feeling of "being behind" naturally exerts a huge amount of stress and burns up a ridiculous amount of energy in any setting. In the practice of law, however, that stressor may be even worse.

It is almost an everyday occurrence in the legal profession to see lawyers, young and old, do a great job for their deserving clients and experience tremendous financial success simply by being involved with the right case on the right date.

When we learn to say "Bravo!" for them—*and really mean it*—then we shed a huge amount of stress. We do not burn energy wishing we were in their shoes or judging ourselves by the success or failure of our peers. We need to learn to allow ourselves to focus completely on who and where we are in this hierarchy of living and lawyering on any given day. We will be much more at ease when we can say with happiness and well-deserved pride, unmitigated by the practices we do not have:

> I am a workers' compensation lawyer in Peoria, Illinois. My clients are depending on me to be the best that I can be. I have no million-dollar jury verdicts. I am not listed in *Who's Who Among Trial Lawyers*. While tomorrow, all of that may change, today I will not stress myself out by judging myself against the success or failure of my peers.

Rarely do we meet someone else's expectations, much less our own. When we get to the point that our own approval of who we are is more important than the approval of others, we will surely abandon one thick layer of stress in our practice, and we will discover a new wealth of energy to devote to both living and practicing law.

The feeling of lack of accomplishment in our profession is not unique to lawyering. However, the negative stress that results seems to be inordinately high in our profession.

HE VALUED TOLERANCE

Just as Atticus understands and accepts where he is in the world, he is constantly trying to understand where others really stand and why they stand there.

One example is an occasion when he is talking with Scout about her need to become more tolerant of other people.

> "First of all," he said, "if you can learn a simple trick, Scout, you'll get along a lot better with all kinds of folks. You never really understand a person until you consider things from his point of view—until you climb into his skin and walk around in it."

We can watch Atticus apply this very principle and also resolve a conflict between what he believes and what others believe. He makes it seem simple.

Perhaps it is. He knows and accepts where he is, and he constantly tries to do the same with others. He seems to recognize that intolerance is much too heavy a burden to bear.

Atticus The Peacemaker

Most of us adapt well to the conflict that is so prevalent in our profession. We recognize that engaging in and confronting conflict are part of our job description. Unfortunately, some of us have adapted and grown too accustomed to conflict as a way of life.

In doing so, we have allowed one of our great skills of peacemaking to atrophy, and we have allowed ourselves to waste a huge amount of energy in the process. Most of us are not judicious enough in our practice and in our lives outside our practice about how and when we should engage ourselves in conflict. We fail to recognize that we have become so comfortable with conflict that we allow it to burn its way into completely inappropriate places in our lives.

Atticus probably deplores conflict although he can confront it when he has to. The difference between him and most of us is that he has not allowed his skill as a peacemaker to weaken. It is evident that, to Atticus, peacemaking is less stressful, uses less energy, and is more effective for him than unnecessary conflict.

For example, shortly after Scout and Jem begin to interact with the reclusive Boo Radley, Boo starts leaving little gifts for them in a hole in one of the Radley trees close to the sidewalk – chewing gum, a broken watch and chain, an old spelling medal, and a boy and a girl carved from soap.

The children decide to write a thank you note and put it in the hole. The next day, the hole has been cemented shut by Boo's keeper, Mr. Nathan Radley. Jem asks Mr. Radley if he put cement in the hole and why, and Mr. Radley says:

"Tree's dying. You plug 'em with cement when they're sick. You ought to know that, Jem."

Children rarely believe our lies, although they try not to contradict us. Puzzled, Jem asks Atticus if the tree is dying. Atticus says,

"Why no, son, I don't think so. Look at the leaves, they're all green and full, no brown patches anywhere."

"It ain't even sick?"

"That tree's as healthy as you are, Jem. Why?"

"Mr. Nathan Radley said it was dyin'."

"Well, maybe it is. I'm sure Mr. Radley knows more about his tree than we do."

Now Atticus could have said to Jem that Mr. Radley was an old fool who does not know diddly. He could have been critical, but he was not. It is clear that he knows Mr. Radley has his reasons for what he has said to Jem. While not ratifying what he knows to be untrue, Atticus has shown Jem a compromise in view that ends an unresolvable conflict between what seems (and even is) true and what human beings convey to one another in oblique, untrue ways.

We as adults know that what Mr. Radley says is his way of telling Jem that Boo is sick and kept inside and that the hole is a leak that is letting him out, so Mr. Radley plugs it. Atticus could have told Jem so, but he allows Jem to learn or reason for himself. All Atticus tells Jem is that "Mr. Radley knows more about his tree than we do." Atticus applies his reason and encourages Jem to learn to do likewise. On the other hand, the conversation could have gone this way. Puzzled, Jem asks Atticus if the tree is dying.

> "Why no, son, I don't think so. Look at the leaves, they're all green and full, no brown patches anywhere."

"It ain't even sick?"

"That tree's as healthy as you are, Jem. Why?"

"Mr. Nathan Radley said it was dyin'."

"Well, you know Mr. Nathan is a damned fool who's keeping his brother locked in the basement. He plugged that hole so Boo couldn't put stuff in it and you'd stop writing notes to Boo. Frankly, Jem, we ought to file suit against Mr. Radley . . . habeas corpus old Boo. I figure we can get Radley for unlawful imprisonment or some such. The very notion of Mr. Nathan thinking he can get between us and Boo offends the hell out of me, and you ought to be offended, too!"

One way, we have the process of peacemaking; the other way, we have escalation of conflict.

We are left with the choice of which avenue we prefer to take dozens of times every day. Atticus appears not in the least offended by Mr. Radley's behavior although it is fairly clear Atticus would not handle his life or problems in the same way the Radleys have handled theirs.

Perhaps in a courtroom Atticus would have to ask Mr. Radley some tough questions. But Atticus is in his home talking to his child. Atticus understands Mr. Radley. He thinks Jem should understand Mr. Radley, so he says, "I'm sure that Mr. Radley knows more about his tree than we do." As attorneys, we are paid to know more about the other man's tree than he does, but in our personal lives, claiming to know more is often counterproductive.

Atticus's role as a peacemaker is a timeless role, one I think many of us would do well to take up again. Abraham Lincoln recognized and praised the art of peacemaking by saying:

> Discourage litigation, persuade your neighbors to compromise whenever you can. Point out to them

> that the nominal winner is often
> the real loser . . . as a peacemaker,
> the lawyer has a superior opportu-
> nity for being a good man.

What enables Atticus to be a peacemaker is that his beliefs are not infringed on by others; he does not suffer from visible frustration or from imputing wrongfulness and intentionality to his family, friends, or neighbors. Atticus is clearly a moral man, but he does not moralize. He does not react with outrage or indignation. He is confident enough in his beliefs that his ego is not offended; that is, he does not let others interfere with those beliefs. He must be *accepting* to be a successful peacemaker.

The most important aspect of Atticus's refusal to "enjoy" or participate in unproductive conflict is that his refusal is totally rational, totally deliberate, and totally successful. This calm and realistic view of life enables Atticus to have expectations that can be met, enables him to teach rather than criticize, and enables him to meet every situation with measured and judicious responses.

He does not internalize conflict.

Unlike many of the bellicose "litigator" types in our profession, he is not afraid of being milder, easier, and more of a peacemaker.

He is not fearful that by being less rigid, less "in your face," he will encourage other people to take advantage of him. He obviously believes the risk is very slight.

Atticus never escalates a conflict precisely because he does not let the conflict get inside of him, and in that way, conflict does not come back out of him magnified.

Fear of Failure—
Another Energy Burner Atticus Avoided

When we chose lawyering as our profession, we allowed ourselves many opportunities to be successful and just as many opportunities to fail. Problem is, our failures often impact the lives of many other people. We put our clients at risk right along with ourselves.

Interviews with attorneys about the topic of failure have led me to believe that fear of failure exacts a heavier toll on our lives than actual failure. Fear of failing smothers our vitality and drains our energy; it paralyzes many of us.

One attorney explains his fear of failure this way:

> When I begin to dwell on the risks I place on myself and my client, I am at my worst as a lawyer. I feel like a deer in the road caught in the light of oncoming traffic. I recognize that I am no longer lawyering when I become so fearful of failure that I do not act, do not take risks.

When we allow our fear of failing ourselves and our clients to overpower our ability to succeed, lawyering has ceased to be fun. There are not enough rewarding hours in the day to offset the disastrous expense of energy such a mindset creates.

Atticus fails at one of the most important cases in his life. He knows he has been set up to fail from the outset. It is not that he has created a self-fulfilling prophecy by accepting his failure, but, rather, he simply understands and accepts the limitations placed on him.

He explains his thoughts to his brother, Jack:

> "I'd hoped to get through life without a case of this kind. But [Judge] John Taylor pointed at me and said 'you're it.'"

Jack says,

> "Let this cup pass from you?"

Atticus responds,

> ". . . Right. . . . You know what is going to happen as well as I do, Jack."

Atticus knows that prejudice and bias are going to dictate the outcome of his case. He knows failure is inevitable but he does his best anyway, without fear or regret.

There is an arrogance that exists in the practice of law that actually intensifies a fear of failure, especially in younger lawyers. Such arrogance is found in the claims of older, more experienced trial lawyers who should know better but are pompous enough to claim seriously they "have never lost at trial." It is also an arrogance generated by the "flash in the pan" trial lawyer who is fortunate enough to be in the right courtroom on the right day with the right jury and the right facts and becomes an "overnight success" in spite of his or her true inability.

Most young trial lawyers do not have the luxury of trying the perfect case. Yet some try to accept only perfect cases or insist on only trying that mythical beast which avoids what they fear greatly, failure.

They eliminate the risk because they believe the consequences of failure are too much to bear. The attorneys who weather isolated failures in their practice are the ones who recognize that there is nothing about the practice of law so magical that it defies the law of averages. The law of averages works for us and against us in the lawyering business the same way it works in any other business.

Fearing failure does not improve those averages one bit. Fear of failure simply creates stress and anxiety that drains our useful energy.

Perhaps the most healthy attitude about failure in the practice of law was shared with me by an immensely successful and respected trial lawyer who has lost far more than he has won.

> I know when I experience disaster after disaster in my practice, whether at trial or in the office, that the law of averages is lining up my way. The pump has been primed for a truly great event to take place for me and one of my clients. I try to be like the little boy who wades through a room full of horse manure looking for a pony.

Whether or not the law of averages truly does line up for him after a string of failures is not really the point here. What is more important is that he recognizes that failure is often a reality. Instead of allowing the reality to create anxiety, he chooses to put it in the most favorable light. For him, each time he fails, the law of averages moves him ever closer to at least one success.

Atticus Had A Healthy Worry Pattern— What Kind Do We Have?

Scout recounts how Atticus worries:

> I sometimes think Atticus subjected every crisis of his life to tranquil evaluation behind the *Mobile Register, The Birmingham News* and the *Montgomery Advertiser.*

The process of worry has a tendency to snowball rapidly in the practice of law. Part of the reason is that we have such a sense of identity with what we do for a living. In other words, most of our waking hours are spent being a lawyer. As a result, once we develop a worry about our practice, that worry engulfs us throughout the day and even into the night because of our myopic focus on our practice.

As noted, Atticus sits in the evening reading his newspapers and also in thought about problems he has to address. Fact is, however, Atticus seems not so much to "worry" as "consider" things calmly.

In the weeks leading up to Tom Robinson's trial, Atticus and his children are subjected to all forms of ridicule by the citizens of Maycomb. Atticus points out to Scout that it is difficult to worry and focus on day-to-day living at the same time. He explains to Scout, "It's not time to worry yet," and also adds, "when summer comes, you'll have to keep your head about far worse things."

In short, Atticus eschews worry as a solution to the kinds of problems that must be confronted head on. He may spend some quiet time in the evenings contemplating problems he and his family face but does not fret over what is unreal or unworthy of his energy.

He picks his allotted time for what might better be called problem solving than what most of us call worry. His two keys are: *He picks a time,* and *he addresses or faces actual problems with a view to reaching a solution.* He does not appear anywhere in the book to be carrying these problems away from this "worry time."

After asking friends of mine to analyze when and how they worry, I was surprised by the interesting and well-defined worry patterns they came up with. For example, one attorney explained that she begins worrying Sunday afternoon about Monday morning regardless of what she has scheduled and regardless of whether there is, in fact, a well-defined problem that she must face on Monday. This worry pattern was so extreme that beginning on Sunday afternoons she would develop some ill-defined notions that Monday was going to be bad.

She began worrying about brush fires before sparks had even kindled the flame. She grew fearful and worried about a whole host of nonspecific bad things that could happen on Monday morning. The good news is that she developed a solution for dealing with Monday's goblins and gremlins:

> She would go by her office, if only for an hour, sometime on Sunday and review her scheduling for the week, organize her desk, and even make calls to difficult clients.

> If she went through this routine early in the morning on Sunday, she found that she did not worry the rest of the day.

Instinctively, she had identified her pattern of worry and then decided on a course of action that required her to do something about it. She arrived at a textbook solution for combating unnecessary and unreasonable worry in her practice through sheer instinct and intuition rather than through instruction, but her solution paid off.

Another example of an attorney who instantly arrived at a way to combat his pattern of worry is the example of one who dealt with what I will refer to as "night terror." Sixty-two percent of all the attorneys who responded to question-naires on the topic of worry stated they "worry in the middle of the night when they should be sleeping."

This particular attorney was no different. His pattern of worry was such that if he awoke for any reason during the night, his mind would be flooded with sometimes real but mostly imag-ined problems in his practice. He found that 90 percent of the worries that drained all of his energy in the night seemed almost absurd in the light of day.

Again, he first identified the fact that there was a pattern to his worry. Next, he realized there was absolutely no action that he could take to solve any problems, real or imagined, in the middle of the night.

More important, however, he took action to modify his pattern of worry. Every day for the first hour of his work day, he wrote down every potential problem that remotely concerned him and then attempted to work through each problem, one by one, throughout the day.

Through this simple routine, he conditioned himself to choose the time when he would worry. Further, he reasoned that it was more beneficial for him to worry in a setting where he had better control.

Most professionals who have written about the process of worry conclude that, statistically, only an extremely low percentage of the issues that we choose to worry about will ever develop as true problems. There are any number of illustrations of how accurate that theory actually is.

For example, some worry specialists suggest that if we were to write down a list of worries every day and place them in a box, when we checked the box at the end of the year, the overwhelming majority of the worry items in there would never have come to pass. One attorney I know wholeheartedly bought into the idea that 90 percent of our worries are completely outrageous and absurd. He recognizes that most worries are based on totally irrational premises, but he indulges himself to visualize the worst that could happen and stands ready to accept it if he must. His philosophy is that once he is capable of accepting the worst that could happen, then worry steals less of his energy.

For example, he might consider and accept that some event in his life might cause him to lose his house, his car, his vacation home, and his membership at his health club, but he will probably be able to hold onto his wife, his children, his good sense, and his ability to make a living somehow. This approach is certainly not original in dealing with worry. It is an approach that has been stated dozens of different ways over the centuries by scholars ranging from Buddha to Norman Vincent Peale.

The law of averages dictates that the vast majority of worries will never develop into realities. Nevertheless, 65 percent of survey respondents said that they worry about their practice at work, 62 percent said that they worry about their practice in the middle of the night, and 54 percent said they worry about their practice even when they are on vacation. Most of us recognize that our worries about our practice are purely a function of our imagination. However, we still allow worry to take its toll and unnecessarily drain our energy.

The good news is that every one of us has a very distinct worry pattern. We must realize that once we honestly analyze our worry patterns, we can make successful adaptations in our daily routines to combat them.

An example of a simple adaptation is that of an attorney who for years knowingly created worry by constantly calling her office whenever she was gone for more than an hour. Her conduct was obsessive to the point that she carried her hand-held telephone everywhere. She knew that when she called the office, there typically was no pressing matter that needed to be handled. While there were no matters that required worry, she was always in search of something to worry about.

This attorney could not sit through a seminar without making two or three calls to the office in search of a worry to indulge. She had always had this worry pattern, but the solution to the problem was simple. She got rid of the tool that helped her worry, her hand-held telephone. And even without her umbilical-cordless phone, she has not been sued for malpractice, she has not been reported for ethical violations, she has not faced financial demise, and Mike Wallace and his *60 Minutes* camera crew have never shown up at her office to "ambush" her.

The happy ending is that she first analyzed the fact that she did have a distinct worry pattern, and second, she adjusted her lifestyle to eliminate that pattern. What she illustrated was that there is a method for dealing with worry.

It is not my method, and it is not a new method. It is a method that people managers have used for decades in training and managing, a method that has been developed by corporate executives who probably deal with far more worry than we do as trial attorneys. This simple approach to correcting worry patterns is:

1. Figure out what your worry pattern is. What time of day or night do you worry? How long do you dwell on particular worries?

2. Write down on paper a specific list of the issues that you worry about. Are they financial issues? Are they deadlines? Are they health issues?

3. Add and subtract from that list, separating true worries from mere annoyances.

4. Prioritize your worry topics.

5. Creatively change that worry pattern. Strategies may include:

   • Choosing a particular time of day for the "task of worry."

   • Committing yourself to limiting the time that you will spend on a particular day allowing yourself to worry.

   • Taking some action, no matter how small or how fruitless it may seem.

- Adapting your thinking to accept the worst if the worst should come.

Beyond Atticus, Can We Grow and Learn?

I think we can build on what we have learned so far. We have seen that there are a great many clues in *To Kill A Mockingbird* about how to deal with the problems of stress and worry, and we have discussed some specifics of how to deal with such things.

If we first deal with stress and worry—energy zappers—we will have both energy and time to deal with the many problems a modern law practice brings, problems Atticus did not encounter.

One of the most common problems trial lawyers want to discuss when they talk about their practices in the '90s is not having enough time and energy to meet adequately all the demands they are faced with in both their practices and their lives.

As we have seen, the two biggest energy drains in the world are stress and worry. Almost no one ever gets worn down or burns out from accomplishment. In fact, every time people get something done, they feel a surge of both spirit and energy. We can convert some of that saved energy to solving nuts-and-bolts problems and be well on the road to living in Maycomb, Alabama, circa 1935, a place where a day seemed to have more than 24 hours, not fewer, as seems to be our lot.

Obviously no single solution will solve every problem. Just as each of us has specific and personal problems, there is no "one size fits all" solution. Luckily, there are all sorts of solutions to all sorts of problems. All we have to do is use them.

WE HAVE PROBLEMS ATTICUS DID NOT HAVE, BUT WE ALSO HAVE TOOLS TO SOLVE THEM

There are problem-solving tools that I believe we can utilize but do not. My survey indicates that far more of us have problems than read motivational or self-help books about how to deal with them. In fact, almost 44 percent of respondents said they never read motivational books.

That seems odd.

Experts, philosophers, and gurus have been analyzing and writing about solutions to life/work problems such as handling worry and stress, conserving energy, and learning effective time management for centuries. For a group of professionals whose reading and comprehension skills are probably above average, it seems we are doing ourselves a huge disservice by discounting the importance of such information.

The best I can tell, ignoring this vast self-help resource leaves a bunch of very smart people out there who are suffering through a life of "hurry sickness," stress, and worry, when a good many of their problems are solvable with a little reading.

Of course, every man or woman is entitled to pick his or her poison. We can ignore our problems if we like, but one of the main problems with such an attitude is that the things that poison us too often spill over into our private lives, into the lives of others.

A key ABA survey answer as to how lawyers deal with the stresses of practice was that 85 percent of us "try to deal with the underlying problem."

That attempt is good news. The bad news is that many of us fail to use all the tools available for solving underlying problems.

It flies in the face of logic and reason that we are unwilling to borrow the insight and intellect of recognized experts on improving quality of life.

CHAPTER FIVE

DEFINING ATTICUS AND OURSELVES FULLY

Harper Lee dedicated her book "for Mr. Lee and Alice in consideration of Love and Affection." If either of these true-to-life people was the model for a character in Harper Lee's book, most of us would certainly be proud to know them. Perhaps Harper Lee showed us only the very best parts of these characters, or perhaps these characters truly understand some truths about living that make them appear bigger than life.

Either way, their creation is our gain if we borrow some of what flows from the end of Harper Lee's pen.

WHAT DID HARPER LEE KNOW ABOUT QUALITY OF LIFE THAT SOME OF US MAY NOT KNOW?

In survey, we are saying such vague things as, "I want a higher quality of life." And, "I spend too much time practicing law and not enough time living, which causes me to be dissatisfied with my practice because the quality of life I have with my family suffers."

We have legitimate complaints that we can list, even define in general terms. In looking at Atticus Finch, we can see that he has few complaints and probably less to complain about, but not because he has no problems. Rather, he deals with them differently than most of us do.

He is able to do so precisely because most of the time he understands both himself and the underlying basis for whatever problems arise Obviously, we need to understand ourselves more completely if we are to serve our own lives fully as well as our clients, families, and communities.

One very clear reason that, in the '90s, we as professionals are not able to do so as well and fully as Atticus Finch is that there is a broad and deep part to the quality of knowledge that Atticus is able to draw upon that many modern attorneys have not taken the time to develop. The "seen that, been there, done that" credo of the '80s and '90s truly emphasizes the idea that we are living in an age that appears to value image or form over substance. Modern philosophers are constantly beating the drum that says we have become shallow by our own choosing.

In an age where more new information and raw data are produced and published in a decade than in all the preceding millennia, many of us have not a clue as to how we fit into the picture. We know all sorts of things, but we do not have time to find out what these things mean. We know more than we feel. We are emotionally disconnected from life to some degree. In the '90s, when we say we have "been there, done that," we are really only engaging in the process of keeping score instead of proclaiming that we have grown spiritually or intellectually.

We probably have far wider interests or possibilities than Atticus Finch or his contemporaries ever could have had. Problem is, this great width does not give us so much opportunity to run deep.

This situation is not totally our fault. There are many reasons. For one thing, the world in general does not seem to overtly value depth of soul coupled with wisdom. These qualities do not sell well, and they cannot be explained in 30-second sound bites. For another, we have been kept busy doing busywork; we know only what we *need to know*. Also, for the most part, our peers in the practice of law are so much like us that we have become somewhat intellectually inbred.

In previous chapters, we have discussed some serious impediments, primarily emotional, such as stress and worry. We come now to some rougher terrain covered with thicker underbrush. Still, these foothills lead to the steeper, but in some ways clearer-cut, climb to the high ground that Atticus occupies.

THE BROAD AND DEEP PART OF ATTICUS THAT MOST OF US AIN'T GOT

I see at least three reasons why lawyers today do not run so broad and deep as Atticus.

Similarity of thought processes among modern lawyers. We have finally learned to "think like lawyers."

Narrowness of a modern compared to a classical education. We have become victims of the *need to know* concept of learning.

Some of us possess brilliance without much insight. We are brilliant technicians; but the scientist's slide rule does not serve the needs of our clients.

If recognition and understanding of the crux of a problem are the first and most important steps in alleviating it, this ground is well worth cutting a path through.

SIMILARITY OF THOUGHT PROCESSES AMONG MODERN LAWYERS

With rare exceptions, we are the end-product of a very rigid and exacting selection process that allows for almost unlimited personal idiosyncrasies and personality variations, but for almost no variance whatsoever in how we reason or think.

Look at us! With few exceptions, we were good students through grade and high schools. If we had not been good students, we would have been far less likely to go to college.

At the college level, we probably made decent grades or we would not even have been considered for admission to most law schools. There is a fair amount of diversity in the undergraduate majors we took, but one further weeding process insured that, whatever our majors, we were capable of, and exhibited a proficiency at, the specific type of analytical thinking measured by the Law School Admissions Test (the LSAT).

Someone, somewhere, suggested that this pre-law school test would be a good indicator of whether or not the law school applicant would do well in law school and beyond. The LSAT, *a mystical and mythical litmus test,* has for decades helped determine who could and could not be trained to think like a lawyer.

We have all known otherwise brilliant college classmates whose diligence, integrity, and character begged for them to become practicing attorneys, whose admission to our ranks doubtless would have honored and enhanced our profession, but who are not with us today.

However glowing their recommendations, however sterling their grade point averages, they are not here for they failed on some portion of the LSAT. Usually, it was not because they could not read and comprehend test material. They failed at what is known as "analytical reasoning," that curiously

Boolean mathematical process of logic that is supposed to demonstrate our "potential."

Atticus has not gone to law school. I suspect he would have passed the LSAT, but I cannot be certain, for his reasoning and logic are far more human and subjective than mathematical and objective. There's no doubt he understood more about the humanities than hard sciences.

In the July/August 1987 issue of the *Florida Bar Journal,* a past president of the Florida Bar, Ray Ferrero Jr. suggests that we have forgotten what Atticus understood. He wrote:

> In the communications audit conducted by Hill & Knowlton for the Bar, the comments of one participant in a focus group summed the feelings of all: "They teach them law in school, not humanity." Our individual challenge in this crisis of change is to retain our humanity, share the warmth of that humanity, and in general humanize the way we work with clients, the pub-

lic and each other. . . . We need to see ourselves in the role of peacemakers, bringing justice where it is lacking, tranquility where there was turmoil, freedom where it was deprived, and rewards where they are due.

Although there are many issues facing the profession today, I sincerely believe the overriding precipitator is what I perceive as a diminished peripheral vision of attorneys in general. The lack of a pervasive sense of mission by individual lawyers, the absence of a sense of rightness and righteousness that transcends self-interest and commercialism, the loss of a sense of calling, an idealism as in a vocation, that gives all our labor its dignity.

An understanding and total awareness of humanity, of human things, human frailty, and human glory—Atticus has these qualities! They are his prime qualities. They are the stuff that Steinbeck novels are made of. Unfortunately, they are not the qualities that are all that important in our quest to learn how to "think like lawyers" in the '90s.

Rick Kuykendall, of Birmingham, Alabama, does most of the hiring in his law firm. He offers these observations:

> Generation X is now sending me their resumes. Their grades are impressive; they passed their bar exams with no trouble, but it is unusualwhen they can comfortably converse about concepts and ideas that should be basic to any classical education. They understand Palsgraf, but struggle with Plato.

In my survey, 89.9 percent of the respondents stated that since they had graduated from law school, they had not enrolled in any nonlegal educational courses at local colleges. Obviously, this response is not a definitive measure of whether any given number have expanded their nonlegal knowledge base.

But adult or continuing education (even "recreational learning") has become a national pastime most of us appear to have missed. Too bad, for in some ways such programs, which are endemic to almost any community today, have goals that appear very Atticus-like.

For example, in my home town, the University of West Florida's continuing education coordinator, Glenn Goltermann, whose outreach programs extend to a special branch in Japan as well as into local business and industry, says his mission is *"to reach new audiences and develop programs which enhance the life of the mind."*

As a group whose inclinations and propensities tend toward "thinking" or "intellectual" activities, this program sounds very much like something we could enjoy. Golterman further notes that today, "enhancing the life of the mind is no longer the sole province of the Aristotelian academy or the monastery, the ivory tower. It has become an everyday necessity—for business and for industry. Concepts such as thinking about thinking—understanding how we think and improving the quality of our thinking are simply tools of survival in most parts of the business world today. Atticus's goal of urging people to think better has as much relevance today as it did in 1930s Maycomb.

Understanding ourselves, how we think about things and act upon that thinking, should be one of our major goals in seeking an improved quality of life.

To think well is particularly important for us, for our main function as trial attorneys is to understand and help others to recover from injury or disaster, to make peace with themselves and the world, and to be made whole. These are typically complex issues that cannot and should not be handled through uninspired routine.

In order to be of any real service to our clients, we must continue to expand the life of our minds beyond the perimeter of simply "thinking like lawyers."

We must learn to think in different languages, in a variety of philosophies, in diverse cultures, in multiple arts. We must bring more to the table than what is brought by our clients or their foes.

We must remember that reading something does not do us much good unless and until we integrate what we have read into the wider practices of our lives. Atticus carries his broader historical and life perspectives into the forum every day and brings them back home each evening.

NARROWNESS OF MODERN vs. CLASSICAL EDUCATION

The narrowness of modern vs. classical education truly appears to have affected us over the latter half of this century. Some of our older colleagues passed through a different stream of education or "school," one broader and deeper than the one flowing in the '90s.

I certainly do not mean to imply that we are not smart people, for we most certainly are. It is just that the difference between what our predecessors knew and what we now know is vast. Most of them were generalists; we are specialists. Indeed, success in the practice of law today almost demands ever narrower specialization.

Many years ago, the great thinker Alfred North Whitehead said, "A great fact confronting the modern world is the discovery of the method of training professionals, who specialize in particular regions of thought and thereby progressively add to the sum of knowledge within their respective subjects." He went on to say this sort of narrowness and specialization, which was such a "godsend" in moving specialized areas forward, "in the future will be a public danger."

That prediction sounds quite dire, describing us as it does. Worse still, Whitehead was a rather sound thinker, not one given to hyperbole. What he was saying reminded me of a line Pete Seeger sang during the turbulent '60s and early '70s—"The Talking Atomic Bomb Blues," or some such. In his song, Seeger explained that the atomic threat scared Einstein, "and when Einstein is scared," Pete sang, "I'm scared."

Whitehead said this trend toward narrowness and specialization "has its dangers. It produces minds in a groove." Now, if Whitehead was worried about that danger, we should at least consider his concerns.

He went on to say:

> To be mentally in a groove is to live in contemplating a given set of abstractions . . . *but there is no groove or abstraction which is adequate for comprehension of human life*[emphasis supplied]. Of course, no one is merely a mathematician, or merely a lawyer. People have lives outside their professions or their businesses. But the point is the restraint of serious thought within a groove. The remainder of life is treated superficially, with the imperfect categories of thought derived from one profession.

Folks, that describes many of us, but not Atticus. He is not only a truly decent man who has chosen to practice law, but he is an erudite and thoughtful person possessing a more classical breadth and depth of education.

He is not in a groove. He possesses an adequate comprehension of life beyond simply the big picture.

We are the product of what I call a "Need to Know" system. We are told what to read, given assignments, and the vast majority of what we have learned is what we "need to know" to accomplish our coursework, to pass our tests, to file our pleadings, or to submit our *prima facie* cases.

Thus, the vast majority of us run in one narrow channel . . . we are lawyers first and foremost, always and forever.

Perhaps that system is why we worry and fear that we are practicing law too much and living too little. Maybe we vaguely see the very problem Whitehead described coming to pass. It has manifested itself in us. We are the future, in the midst of the danger he was describing.

Whitehead cited several other "dangers arising from this [narrowing] aspect of professionalism" to democratic societies:

> The directive force of reason is weakened.
>
> The leading intellects lack balance.
>
> They see this set of circumstances, or that set, but not both sets together.
>
> In short, the specialized functions of the community are performed better and more progressively, but the generalized direction lacks vision.
>
> This criticism of modern life applies throughout, in whatever sense you construe the meaning of a community. It holds if you apply it to a nation, a city, a district, an institution, a family, or even an individual.
>
> The point is that the discoveries of the nineteenth century were in the

direction of professionalism, so that we are left with no expansion of wisdom or with greater need of it.

I do not think there are many of us who can say that our education, followed by on-the-job training as lawyers and the rigors of practice itself, have not forced us into what Whitehead called "the groove."

If we are to broaden ourselves, acquire balance and vision, become more like Atticus, we are going to have to do exactly what *To Kill A Mockingbird* tells us Atticus does. He educates himself. We must continue to educate and expand ourselves. We must abandon our "need to know" way of thinking and acquire a "want to know" approach.

I have no measure of who has read or studied what in the course of their lives beyond law school. But as I mentioned above, the answer 80.9 percent of survey respondents chose for the statement, "Since the time I graduated from law school, I have enrolled in nonlegal educational courses in local colleges," was "Never"!

Professionals in that group do not sound intent on rounding out their intellectual lives.

The specialization among lawyers has become even more narrow than it was a mere few decades ago when the vast majority of this country's lawyers practiced a little bit of all sorts of law, very much as Atticus does.

Specialization narrows our practices and even our lives outside our practices to some degree. If one practices nothing but domestic law, one might think the world was nothing but one big home brawl. A lawyer who tries nothing but criminal cases might believe the world is nothing but one huge cops-and-robbers crime circus. If one does nothing but attack perfidious manufacturers, one may come to see the world of manufacture as a totally evil one.

The 76.2 percent of us who say we long to "improve our quality of life" perhaps are saying that we recognize we have fallen into the groove Whitehead was concerned about—a groove that is inconsistent with a higher quality of life.

As the old man on the up-country Alabama porch told the lost traveler: "You can't get there from here. You'll have to go somewhere else to start."

Backtracking in order to broaden and deepen our overall education and outlook is one of those "somewhere else" things I believe we all can benefit from.

There is a great deal of truth to the idea that a law school education scares you to death the first year, works you to death the second year, and bores you to death the third year. It is that third year where we become too comfortable with the idea that we have "made it." We have succeeded with our "need to know" education.

There is good reason to believe that we have learned to "think like lawyers."

From that third year on, we begin dedicating ourselves to the art of lawyering 250 hours a month. Our growth as businessmen and technicians begins. We are on our way to possessing brilliance without the human insight that a lawyer like Atticus Finch exhibits or that many of the classic names in law possessed.

We all know the names—Roscoe Pound, Clarence Darrow, Learned Hand, Oliver Wendell Holmes, and Charles P. Curtis. If we know and understand much about these great lawyers, we probably recognize that we respect their human insight as much as we appreciate their intellect. In almost every writing, speech, opening, and closing of these great lawyers, it is evident that they understood the importance of walking around in another man's skin. Their writings weave logic, intellect, and humanity, almost all of which they developed well beyond law school. I doubt they ever arrived at a time in their lives when they stopped growing or when they determined that their understandings and insights were complete.

I suspect there was never a time when they determined that at last they had learned to "think like lawyers."

Chapter Six

Atticus and Ourselves as Hierarchies

The majority of us label ourselves Type A personalities. One of the less conspicuous undesirable results of that kind of personality is that we often stay too busy overachieving to take inventory of how well we are carrying on our nonlawyer roles and relationships. In fact, many of us might find that we approach lawyering at full blast all the time because our profession, in our minds, justifies and excuses our lack of attention in our nonlawyer roles.

All of us have an assortment of roles that are component parts of our lives. We place those roles into a loose hierarchy and seldom evaluate or reevaluate how well that hierarchy is working.

The hierarchy at work in Atticus can be analyzed by building a schematic to represent the systems he as a human being has working in his life.

Unfortunately, such a schematic of our own lives can tell us very little about the *quality or lack thereof* in how the human "machine" operates. It is merely an inventory form. We have to decide what quality we have in the boxes of our hierarchy or what quality we do not have but want to insert.

I started with Atticus Finch, who represents a person whose components and functions seem to be up and running. If Atticus were a motorcar, we would say he runs smoothly on paved road or rutted mudtrack.

What I eventually arrived at was this diagram:

ATTICUS FINCH
Represents Quality of Life as well
as Unity of Self and Purpose
Components and Functions

COMPONENTS
Physical - Intellectual - Emotional
Body - Mind - Spirit

FUNCTIONS
Private Person
Public Person

PRIVATE

PUBLIC

Father

Family Man

Friend

Neighbor

Legislator

Citizen

Lawyer

PHYSICAL

Health

Fitness

INTELLECTUAL

Worry

Motivation

EMOTIONAL

Fear

Stress

Anger

SPIRITUAL

Beliefs

Faith

I think we can use such a personal schematic as a tool for understanding, then restructuring, our own components and functions to achieve the higher-quality lives we desire.

For example, if after devising such a schematic for ourselves we recognize that our role as parent is not operating as smoothly as we wish, then we are on to the road to discovering why. Do we fail because we don't apply our intellect to that relationship? Do we bring too much emotion, or not enough? Do we smother that relationship with anger or stress? Does our role as lawyer interfere with that relationship?

Once we visualize on paper how many roles we play in our lives beyond lawyering, we can then determine how well those other roles are functioning.

All of us who practice law have the same components as Atticus or similar ones. The state of one's components is going to have an obvious effect on whether one functions well or even at all. If our components seem heavily loaded with negative traits as compared to positive ones, it is clear that we will function badly at the top level that we label "quality of life" or "unity of self and purpose."

For example, an angry, stress-ridden, fearful lawyer would hardly be functioning at peak potential, nor would an emotionally distressed parent, friend, or neighbor be in top form.

That is to say, when we logically, rationally, and intellectually see our component parts and functions, all we are seeing is potential. When we add feelings, emotions, behavior—all sorts of intangibles that each of us brings to our individual boxes—we have our lives in motion, in action. How we feel and act within this schematic tells us whether our lives possess or lack quality.

Many self-help books suggest writing things down as a helpful exercise. I believe each of us can benefit from writing down or laying out our own lives in a rational hierarchy.

Doing so will enable us to begin adding notes concerning the feelings and/or behaviors that define whether we are achieving the quality of life we want and deserve. Each of us can isolate and write down the areas where we have problems.

Cold, hard, written-in-stone problem areas should leave each of us with no confusion about which of our functions or component parts needs attention.

The Problem with Functions Is . . .

Functions (some might call them "roles") are neither good nor bad; they simply exist. For the most part, we choose our functions or roles. We chose to be lawyers. If married, we chose to be married the same way most of us determined whether or not to be parents.

All of these "functions" are interactive, either with social institutions or people over whom we have little or no control. I would not bother to say the following except we are all familiar with the tendency to miss the obvious while looking for some deeper or more complex meaning.

As you add boxes to your chart of functions, or merely study Atticus' basic chart, you will recognize immediately how sketchy it is, how much more complex our lives really are than a simple hierarchical schematic can show. These boxes at another level or two down could become totally unmanageable, geometric progression at its worst!

If we were describing a machine, we could not run it or keep it functioning properly if we were anything short of magicians. We could add and delete boxes, people, interactions, duties, and obligations that go along with these functions until we were down to being hermits who interacted only with pure nature. Even then we could not count on nature to be fully cooperative.

And, if we are honest with ourselves, we would simply have to admit we really have little or no control over how these same or similar functions that are going on in others will work or operate at the points where we interact with them.

I believe we are now at the crux of the matter we want to understand more fully.

First, Atticus always seems to understand where he is in his own complex hierarchy of components and functions. He knows what is working well at any given moment and within most situations.

Second, he appears highly aware that everyone else in his universe brings to any interaction his or her own hierarchical structure influenced by whether his or her components are hitting on all cylinders or malfunctioning.

Third, Atticus understands that the only thing he can control is what he will bring to each of these interactions. He chooses to bring only the very best of himself to them, and, moreover, to ascribe to others their very best, however rough and tentative their best may be.

He understands both his own limitations and theirs in adjusting this interaction. He understands fully that no one "masters" or controls the almost mystically mysterious moment when humans make contact for better or worse.

He recognizes what we apparently do not: There is no magic MasterCard that we can whip out and use to buy mastery of our destiny and control the destiny of others when our hierarchies interact with theirs. What we can do is ensure that our behavior and applied reason do not do more harm than good.

We can do what Atticus does. Insofar as it is possible for others, he helps them see for themselves in what direction the higher ground lies. Atticus does not concern himself with how well he can command or control; instead, he focuses on how well he can gently influence. The best example of his power to influence comes when Scout is explaining to her elementary school teacher that, yes, she does know how to read, but no one has ever *taught* her how.

Scout does recall, however, that for as long as she can remember, Atticus put her up in his lap every evening read the newspaper to her.

> I could not remember when the lines above Atticus' moving finger separated into words, but I had

stared at them all the evenings in my memory, listening to the news of the day, Bills to Be Enacted into Laws, the diaries of Lorenzo Dow —anything Atticus happened to be reading when I crawled into his lap every night. Until I feared I would lose it, I never loved to read. One does not love breathing.

Atticus chooses not to "be in control" of his interaction with Scout. He merely seeks to have a gentle influence within that interaction.

I think this truth is a tough one for most of us to swallow. The realization that we do not and cannot gain mastery or control over situations poses special problems for those of us who are lawyers, for controlling or directing events is our business. When situations are out of control, they are potentially damaging to our clients and ourselves. Creating or bringing order out of chaos is at the very core of our profession. Therefore, we try to convince ourselves that we can and should bring order and control to all of our interactions. We cannot.

The main part of what *we* can control is *what we bring* to the interactions in our lives.

DO WE KNOW WHAT IS GOOD AND WHAT IS NOT?

When viewing his or her "hierarchy" of components and functions, I do not think there is anyone who does not know or cannot tell what is good and what is not.

As you do this hierarchy exercise, treat yourself to the same kind of rational and questioning analysis you would give a client's case or an opponent's brief. For example, we know that fear, anger, and stress are primarily emotional and that worry is basically an intellectual activity, but we know, too, that they interact and that all of them carry a very real physical price—whether in lost sleep, poor health, or even the classic heart attack that "hurry sickness" can cause. In this way you will isolate and define your own more pressing problems.

If stress in the emotional component causes

you to be a less effective lawyer or a less effective parent, friend, or neighbor, you will want to exchange stress for a positive emotional component.

How you do such things will, of course, depend on the problem and your personality.

Atticus Is a Hierarchy, but People Are More Than the Sum of Their Parts

Lawyers are by both education and experience inclined to break things down into rational hierarchies. We do it in cases. We often analyze clients, fixing on certain traits or facets of their existence; to some extent we compartmentalize everything and everyone. For example, we pigeonhole items—a letter goes in the correspondence file; evidence goes in the evidence bin; testimony goes with the deposition or testimony file.

What we often overlook in dealing rationally in hierarchical fashion is that absolutely every system on earth somehow is more than the sum of its parts. We might call this little bit of extra stuff *quality*.

A bright red sports car speeding through a curve at Sebring at dawn is quality striking the eye, moving the soul of one who loves cars—momentarily revealing speed, grace and a misty morning touched with the faint hues of impending sunrise. This scene may even send a shiver up one's spine. The same event may leave another person totally indifferent or unmoved. Obviously, one person may see quality in the event; another may be blind to it.

An old Armenian proverb states that "Hell is a stylish shoe," implying the sin of vanity in its wearer. Yet a stylish shoe that sets off an unfinished outfit may bring pleasure to those who view the person wearing it and lift the wearer's spirits, lending an aura of quality.

Quality itself usually results when the various facets of ourselves—physical, mental and emotional—coincide or agree. Quality is the light bulb going on above the head of the cartoon character who suddenly understands what something really is, not what he or she mistakenly thought it was.

I think this premise is important because Atticus Finch is a very understanding lawyer and human being. Atticus understands that people are dynamic hierarchies made up of complex components and functions that, taken together, are more than the measurable sum of their parts. Our tendency as rational professionals is to see certain facets of human hierarchies while failing to understand or acknowledge that we are dealing with total packages. This point of view is very limiting.

In *To Kill A Mockingbird,* that point-of-view appears through what we might call "Aunt Alexandra" thinking. Her narrower, more myopic assessment of others makes for a very simple, easy-to-deal-with world. And, that is how it is so long as you live in a self-contained, self-centered, limited world. Too bad most of us do not have the luxury of living there, for ignorance obviously can be bliss. Let's look at this limiting behavior for a minute.

Because his children are growing up and need a feminine hand, Atticus invites his sister, Alexandra, to live with them. Who is she?

> Aunt Alexandra was one of the last of her kind: she had river-boat, boarding-school manners; let any moral come along and she would uphold it; she was born in the objective case; she was an incurable gossip. When Aunt Alexandra went to school, self-doubt could not be found in any textbook, so she knew not its meaning.

Aunt Alexandra judges everyone by her own standards, not theirs. It frustrates and infuriates her when she recognizes that she has little command or control over the way families, groups or individuals around her act. Alexandra shows no interest in influencing others either positively or negatively. Her recognition of her lack of control instead causes her to view others as aberrations. She pigeonholes each of these aberrations or, as Scout says:

Aunt Alexandra, in underlining the moral of young Sam Merriweather's suicide, said it was caused by a morbid streak in the family. Let a sixteen-year-old girl giggle in the choir and Aunty would say, "It just goes to show you, all the Penfield women are flighty. Everybody in Maycomb, it seemed, had a Streak: a Drinking Streak, a Gambling Streak, a Mean Streak, a Funny Streak.

Once, when Aunty assured us that Miss Stephanie Crawford's tendency to mind other people's business was hereditary, Atticus said, "Sister, *when you stop to think about it* [emphasis added], our generation's practically the first in the Finch family not to marry its cousins. Would you say the Finches have an Incestuous Streak?"

Atticus views people as flexible hierarchies; "Aunty" views them purely as boxes, rigidly fixed by heredity. If we think like Aunty, we will spend more time interacting ineptly within our practices and lives than we do interacting calmly and realistically.

What we see again is that Atticus does *"stop to think about it."* He applies reason and brings understanding and insight to all his interactions. The fact that Aunty's theory of heredity and "streaks" is based on lumping all members of any family class into the same category amuses Atticus rather than disturbs him. No doubt he recognizes that Aunty's thinking is the rule, not the exception for most people.

Chapter Seven

Problems We Have That Atticus Didn't

Both my survey and the ABA's suggest we have at least some common concerns that are simply business management problems. Those problems generally are:

> We need to take more time from our practices to broaden and enrich our lives and the lives of our families, but we claim we do not have the time.

We approach our work in various ways, not all of which are well thought out, productive, or rewarding. We are suffering from time famine, but the problem is curable.

If we divide our day-to-day living into three time segments, those segments would separate as follows:

- Time for work or professional life.

- Time for personal or family life.

- Time for sleep.

These segments add up to 168 hours a week, 8,736 hours a year. Every study ever done about lawyers shows we work long hours, 200 to 240-plus hours a month. The usual studies fail to add all the personal, family, or sleep time lost to thinking or worrying about our work. For example, here is the breakdown:

> *65.8% said they worry mostly while they are at work.*

62.1% said they worry in the middle of the night.

44.7% said they even worry while on vacation.

Only 27.3 percent said, *"I seldom worry about my practice."*

All this says one thing: Our chief problem is we do not balance our time properly among work, personal, and sleep areas. Most of us say we know this is because our work has overrun our personal and sleep lives.

In previous chapters, we said we needed to learn to understand and manage ourselves a bit better, and if we have done so even to a small degree, we should have a bit more energy. Next, we must apply that energy rationally in gaining better control of our businesses by learning to manage our working *time.*

If we are in fact able to recoup any energy at all by adjusting the way we view ourselves and the work around us, then we want to use that new-found energy rationally. Applying personal energy rationally begins with understanding how we misuse time.

ATTICUS IS A ONE-MAN SHOW—
MOST OF US ARE A THREE-RING CIRCUS

The logical place to look for and free up time is in the business segment of our practices.

Look at it this way: Even a one-lawyer show today has a secretary, maybe two, a legal assistant, an accountant, and other personnel—full or part time—to help her or him "manage" the load.

Most trial lawyers today, especially those involved in complex litigation, are by necessity running fairly large "businesses." Whatever size practice, we have expenses, we have payrolls, we have personnel (and personnel problems), we have budgets, libraries, active files to keep up with, and massive closed files to store and maintain. We have phones, Dictaphones, pagers, cell-phones, faxes, and who knows what.

All of the above has to be maintained and paid for. Not surprisingly, some 53.4 percent say one of the most significant fears they have is of "not generating enough business."

At times it seems to some of us that we practice law almost as a sideline to this huge hog of a business. If there is a single absolute difference between all of us and Atticus Finch, it may be that we are, and must be, both lawyers and business managers in a limited amount of time. My question is, how can we manage something we do not understand? The answer is, we cannot.

LET'S LOOK AT HOW WE MANAGE THE BUSINESS END OF OUR PRACTICES

According to my survey, the following describes how we approach our work:

72.2% — I am most productive in short spurts throughout the day.

69.8% — I am good about returning phone calls.

68.6% — *I do things in order of importance.*

59.2% — *I dictate answers to mail within three days of the time I receive it (i.e., over 40% of us do not).*

35.5% — *I put tough decisions off as long as possible.*

32.0% — *I am a good organizer (i.e., nearly 70% of us are not).*

22.5% — *My desk is generally well organized.*

5.9% — *I delegate too much.*

3.6% — *I am fearful of returning calls because of what my client might say.*

"The following best describes the way I approach my work schedule:"

53.5% — 8:00 a.m. to 6:00 p.m. Monday through Friday / Part day Saturday and Sunday.

20.9% — 8:30 a.m. to 5:00 p.m. Monday through Friday / Part day Saturday.

16.3% — I vary my schedule; often I take off during the day and work 5:00 p.m. till 10:00 p.m., otherwise my schedule is basically 8:00 a.m. to 5 p.m. Monday through Friday.

9.3% — 8:00 a.m. to 5 p.m. most days but typically I take 1/2 day off between Monday and Friday.

"The following best describes the way I approach my job day to day":

51.1% — I have no specific time set aside to perform particular tasks day to day.

33.3% — I let my secretary do my

scheduling for appointments; depo-
sition, etc., and then I peform repeti-
tive daily tasks as best I can around
that scheduling throughout the day.

1.1% — I set a specific time for
peforming particular tasks: such as
returning all my calls; completing all
my dictation; talking to adjusters,
etc.

From a time and business management analysis, the above responses say that we are making our lives more difficult because of the way we fail to manage our practices.

Most of us let the fight come to us rather than taking the fight to our office wars. There is a management concept or rule of thumb that most upper level people managers try to live by: *Do not Let Type "A" personalities devise or manage time schedules for corporate organizations.* Let the Type B personalities do that because Type A's are terrible about compartmentalizing and performing repetitive tasks with any sense of order and consistency.

The bad news is that nearly 70 percent of us are Type A, or at least believe we are. As a result, our poor time management skills cause our quality of life to suffer greatly.

Responses illustrate that the most difficult process we go through as trial lawyers is defining all the work we have to do and then fitting the process of living around it.

If we want to improve our quality of life, it seems much more logical to define how we want to live and then build our work habits around that schedule for living.

Very few of us address our time management problems by looking ahead for an entire year, for example, and figuring out how much time we want off, when we want to be with our families, how much time we want to ourselves to grow as people. We do not try to manage our time for a year in advance, and you would be floored by the numbers of us who do not even regularly try to manage our time a month in advance.

Most trial lawyers by nature are not bean counters who live and die by the clock. We, as a group, can and should have complete control over how and when we want to work and how and when we want to live just like most of the rest of the world.

It is significant that most respondents who said that they vary their schedule—those who sometimes take off during the day and work 5:00 p.m. until 10:00 p.m.—overall had a better attitude about the practice of law than other respondents.

These were the same people who said that they set a specific time for performing particular tasks such as returning calls, completing dictation, and so forth. They were not the ones who let their secretary schedule appointments at random and then tried to perform daily tasks around those appointments. These were people who demanded that they maintain control of how and when they wanted to work and live. They have a schedule for both. The only way to devise a schedule that amounts to *time management for living* and not just working is to write it down.

Plan it. Put it on paper.

First, you have to arrive at the decision of how many hours you are willing to work each week. If it is 50 or 60 hours, begin with that framework, but then define when it is you do not want to do this 50–60 hours of work.

List your priorities for time to live by deciding when you want to spend time at home with family or time to pursue your hobbies or to grow as a person, to become a broader and deeper person. We know Atticus has his reading and quiet time schedules, divides his time wisely, knows when he is coming and going. Is there any reason why his time management does not make good sense in the '90s?

Only after you have put these priorities in black and white on paper should you begin planning when and how your work life should take place. What I am telling you is that Atticus writes his own life and we can do the same. Even if you think this process is a waste of time because no-way, no-how, are you going to be able to live your ideal time division, do it anyway. Call it your fantasy schedule; call it pure fiction. Call it anything you want, but do it, and you are eventually going to find people calling you at home with your family or in Rio at Carnival if that is where you want to spend your newly freed-up time.

What I am saying is that once you see with honesty and accuracy where you are time-wise and have written down where you would be if you had your way, your way may not seem as unrealistic as you now think.

An attorney I have known for many years had a phenomenal way of approaching this time-for-living "problem." His method certainly did not interfere with his success as an attorney or his ability to do an outstanding job for his clients. He retired at 42 and plans to go back to work at 60. His typical schedule involved 50-hour weeks.

He might work a regular daytime schedule Monday, work Tuesday night, work 15 hours Wednesday, then take Thursday off. He often worked at home and even on his sailboat. His unusual schedule presented absolutely no problems for him from a professional standpoint. He is a writer, an ATP qualified pilot, an offshore sailboat racer, a boat builder, an artist, and the father of two very grateful children. With all that he is still a financially successful attorney.

I might add he did not make this lifestyle adjustment only after he became successful. He lived around his own creative time management schedule throughout most of the time he practiced law.

ATTICUS'S EXAMPLE PROVES UNDERSTANDING LEADS TO LIVING

Part of maximizing your living time is to understand better what you are doing with your time when you are at work. One way is to take a day off and do nothing but analyze and accurately depict how you spend your time. That day will be one of the most productive you have ever spent. What you learn will enable you to understand truly the difference between how you spend your time now and how you would like to spend your time in the future.

Begin by making an exhaustive list of every task you perform while you are at work: answering mail, preparing for depositions, preparing inter-rogatories, preparing complaints, talking to adjust-ers, talking on the phone, etc. Honestly write down everything you do (give yourself realistic time limits just as an insurance company might set time/task limits for a defense lawyer).

Then analyze how you approach each task from the standpoint of how you might improve the time management process. For example, when I listed my tasks, I found that I was handling my mail two or three times rather than once and taking imme-diate action. I found I was spending 15 minutes on phone calls that should have taken seven.

Martin Levin, one of my partners, took a look at his office time management several years ago and came up with these conclusions:

> I found that I was not compartmen-
> talizing daily tasks such as sorting

and acting on mail, dictating pleadings and letters, and returning phone calls. I was leapfrogging from task to task, causing problems:

- It was difficult to focus and concentrate completely on any one task.

- I found I was only truly productive in short spurts throughout the day because juggling multiple tasks is exhausting no matter what you are doing.

- I was wasting time in a wholesale way because I never had a plan for approaching the day. And I never put acceptable time limits on various tasks.

I had no set day for depositions. No set day or time for new clients. No preferred day for hearings.

I simply responded to time demands

as they came up. Further, I had no sense of how long I should devote to a particular task. Should I spend an hour answering phone calls? Should I spend 40 minutes dictating inter-rogatories? I never gave myself any relative time frames.

Once I understood this clearly, there was no way I was going to keep on doing it. I didn't need to be a rocket scientist to know there had to be ways I could run my schedule rather than let it (or my secretary) run me.

MAKING MAYCOMB TIME OUT OF OVERTIME— THINGS WE HAVE TO DO THAT ATTICUS DIDN'T

Just as we see Atticus's chickens come home to roost and mealtime bounty heaped on his back doorstep, we have seen some chickens of our own come home to roost. They are constantly eating up our time. Just about every time management book or magazine article ever written agrees that our time is used up doing the following:

- Things we "must do"
- Things we "should do"
- Things we "would do"

There are sanctions or penalties for failing to do *must do* things; lesser, but still significant, penalties for failing to do those things we *should do*; and very little disadvantage accruing from failing to do things we *would do* if there were time.

Also, there are positive rewards in relative proportion to performance in each category. The quality of life we have depends almost totally on how we use our time.

Essential Time Management Comes in Two Distinct Flavors

There is work time, and there is family or personal time. Both are *must do* and *should do,* in varying degrees. We cannot have the quality of life we all say we want if we do not consider both essential and treat them as such.

The *would do* or "Item 3" element is the wash-the-car, clean-the-garage, buy-a-new-suit type stuff. You can even put off changing the oil in your car for a while without blowing the engine.

The process of time management is much like the process of trying to eat balanced meals. We need to be concerned about eating all the basic food groups. In order to do so, we'd better like, or learn to like, beets, broccoli, carrots, and squash since those are the *must do* foods. Meat and potatoes are the *should do* foods, and key lime pie is the *would do* food. If those food groups stay out of balance for too long, our body suffers.

The same holds true with the process of proper balance in *must, should,* and *would do* items in our working lives. If they are out of balance too long, our lives suffer.

If we have a filing deadline or a case to try, preparation for these things is an absolute *must do.* If a deposition is scheduled, we must attend it. If a response to a set of interrogatories is due, we must prepare it. We must respond to those items on our plate that absolutely require our attention.

Beyond those requirements, there are plenty of *should do* items such as return phone calls and answer correspondence. The sooner we get these things done, the better off we are.

There is no doubt that things we *would do* come in any number of guises, or better put, *disguises*. Quite often, from lack of paying attention or being unaware, we let these things ride on the *should do* serving cart, or even among the *must do* items of our work menu.

Lack of a clear understanding of which of these items is which leads to some awful cases of indigestion. Our survey makes abundantly clear that many of us have indigestion and ulcers from bad feeding habits in the workplace.

Managing Time Is the Art of Gaining Control!

We have only 168 hours per week to keep our lives rolling. Some attorneys are tremendously successful at making that time work, but most are not. The major difference between those who can and those who cannot is that the former control their work lives, the latter are shoved through their work lives willy-nilly by seemingly "uncontrollable forces."

It is impossible to gain control over *must do's, should do's,* and *would do's* without a plan that places you in control. We're wasting time. We're losing our lives, piecemeal. Unless we stop for at least long enough to evaluate which category or where on any given list tasks should be, we may lose more time hopping around from buffet to buffet than we can possibly blow in making lists.

When we chose to be trial lawyers, we placed ourselves at the glutton's table when it comes to eating up time, and since we cannot make more time, the only possibilities left for us are:

• Work more and have less "time off."

• Make the time we spend working more effective and productive, thereby re ducing the amount of time we must spend at work.

Both avenues could be considered time management, but only one allows us to improve our quality of living. It makes sense to analyze how we can make our working time more effective and productive.

NEVER PUT MORE ON YOUR PLATE THAN YOU CAN EAT

If our daily work load or overall case load constitutes our working menu, then the most important thing for us to know and keep in mind is exactly how much we can realistically expect to handle. We need to decide how many hours we wish to work but also decide *when we want to work* and how we want to distribute or redistribute our time. The amount of time we must spend working varies widely and depends on such factors as how efficient or organized we are, how much staff or associate support we have or can acquire, and how much we can intelligently commit ourselves to do.

ABA studies show that between 1984 and 1990, the number of lawyers working more than 240 hours a month increased more than threefold.

Those working between 200 and 239 hours a month also rose from 31 percent to 37 percent. Somewhat naturally, those working mere 40–50-hour weeks declined significantly.

Vacations taken compared to time allowed declined. That is to say, the clear trend, apparently continuing, is this: Lawyers worked longer and harder and took less vacation time between 1984 and 1990.

These are the time pressures lawyers live with. Do they have a negative effect? Is the problem worth making a concerted effort to solve? I think it is, but let me quote the ABA's conclusions:

> First, working long hours has a cumulative effect. People can handle time deprivation for a year or two, but as the years go on and there is no relief, the impact on an individual's psyche increases. Second, there are many people who say lawyers have always had to work hard to get ahead. While that may to a certain extent be true, that

statement does not take into consideration the changed nature of the hours worked. The pressures and demands of law firms and clients, the element of speed created by the advent of fax machines and computers, and the increasing lack of courtesy between lawyers—to name just a few of the factors that create strain for lawyers—have together changed the quality of the hours worked so that 200 hours in today's practice is far more stressful than 200 hours in the late 1960s.

"Well, so what?" you say. "We expected to work like dogs when we set up in practice or joined a firm, didn't we?" Yes, we did. That a trial lawyer has to work long and hard likely will never change. Does this mean we cannot adjust "long" to "shorter" and "hard" to "easier?" Does it mean that putting more on our plates than we can eat should be the norm rather than the exception?

I don't think so.

The pressures and time constraints of our lives will not change if we do not take positive steps to recognize when enough is enough. Most of us have far too much going on in our work lives ever to develop a quality personal life.

That sad fact is completely attributable to our unwillingness—our fear of saying enough is enough. Saying no takes courage when you are constantly fearful that you might miss an opportunity. For some of us, saying no is close to an impossibility, largely because of the way we have been taught or socialized.

So, if we are unwilling to say no or unable to say no because saying yes has become too much of a habit, then we should consider prioritizing the importance of things we pile on our plate.

LISTS OR PRIORITIES MAY BE THE KEY

We quite often do not know, or have not made a conscious effort to decide, what should go where in our three basic categories of *must, should,* and *would do.* Because of that, things ought to be on our *would do* list wind up on our *must do* list and vice versa.

As with everything else we have discussed, I think we have to write these things down. We know this, for one of the most essential tools we have and use is our calendar. That's a "list" we all maintain, but sometimes our calendar simply is not enough. How we put things on our calendar, what days and times for what kinds of things, perhaps should be rethought.

Appointments should have their priorities just as any other part of our workload must be prioritized—*must do, should do, would do.* Yet, according to my survey, many of us let our secretaries fill in almost any blank on our calendar with whoever happens to call or whatever happens to fly by.

On the other hand, I know trial lawyers who are capable of keeping track of almost anything in their heads, including having a sense of priority for every phase of activity in their lives. If you are not one of them, then you will have to write down what you *must, should,* or *would do* for any given time frame. We call this process making and keeping lists.

Lists are not for the feeble-minded alone. Lists are an excellent tool for figuring out where the time is bleeding out of your work and personal life. At the end of a month, a list will tell you where you need to make adjustments in how you spend your time. There are, of course, people who are list crazy, people who waste so much time making lists that the process becomes counter-productive. I am not suggesting you join their ranks.

What I am suggesting is that there are some things you already know you *must do* today, some you know you *should do* this week, and even some you have on your mind that you *would do* this month. Simply put these things down on paper as a well-planned list. Prioritize that list and assign a day or week when you are going to complete each item on your list.

In an ideal world, we would be able to deal with each item on our list in its proper order relative to importance of category and in descending order of importance. In the imperfect world we live in, it may be that numbers one through five under *must do* cannot be done first thing today. But, if item six can be done, it must be done and be checked off the list.

It is only when we have done whatever we *must do* that we should move on to the *should do* list. Take care of a s*hould do,* consider whether it is time to handle another *must do,* then repeat the process. It is only when we have handled what can be handled in each item in the top two that we move downward to the *would do* pile.

You will find a great deal of satisfaction in being able to run your pen through a *must do* item as you complete it. As you cross off the *should do* items, you are moving closer to gaining control of your work schedule rather than allowing it to control you.

Give this simple process a shot for two to three months. You will notice a pattern to what your work life looks like on paper. Once you recognize that there is a pattern, improvement and adjustments become possible. Next, we must delegate what we can.

Sometimes the art of delegation is the only solution to more effective time management. Delegation is absolutely not something you do and forget about. If it is, you have lost touch with what you have delegated. With the absolute certainty of Murphy's First Law this lapse will come back to haunt you.

The ability to delegate is an office art of the first rank, yet many of us neither understand it nor utilize it to fullest advantage.

Certainly, we all delegate many things: "Diana, will you pull X file and have it on my desk tomorrow morning?" "Joe, can you get me a memo this afternoon on the state of the law concerning Y?" Many of these things are routine. The questions we might need to ask are:

- Are there further things that we can delegate to others and feel confident they will be done, properly and on time?

- Can I turn loose and stop believing that I have to have my hands on every detail, my finger in every pie? Can I relinquish control temporarily?

Delegation requires a fine memory and a sense of schedule. Despite the fact that most of us have good memories, I suggest we acquire and keep current a delegation calendar for important delegated things that aren't immediately pending. I'd be a fool to write down in this tome, "Diana is supposed to have X file on my desk in the morning." I would note, however, that I expect a brief I have delegated to an associate (one due to be filed three weeks from now) to be on my desk in time for me to revise it if I have to.

The absolute heart of successful delegation boils down to three simple things: *assign or delegate; fix a date or time for performance; follow up*.

INTERRUPTIONS KEEP ME FROM WORKING EFFECTIVELY

Clearly time is more effectively utilized when

we concentrate. All of us know that interruptions or distractions greatly increase the amount of time it takes us to do things. Indecision, too many tasks at once, jumping from one thing to another eat up time to no purpose.

I asked a handyman electrician/plumber/carpenter type why his rates were so high for such a small amount of work actually done on a job. He explained that the customer has to pay for him to load his van, drive over, take out and hook up his tools, do the work, however brief, pick up his tools and put them away, clean up after himself, and clear out.

The same holds true for us. We pay for all the setup work we perform and re-perform in order to catch up to where we were before we were interrupted (or before we jumped off to another unrelated task on our own hook).

Ken Bailey, a trial lawyer in Houston, Texas, explained that he applies these simple rules to beginning and finishing day-to-day tasks around his office.

If you start something and can finish it, do so.

If not, do absolutely everything you can before putting it down.

If you put it down, set a time or place to pick it up again, and write down or list that time and place.

If you know you will not have time to finish or significantly enhance a project or piece of work, don't waste setup time starting on it until you do.

Never begin a less important task until you have finished the more important task.

I Can't Put Everyone Off, Can I? Or, Making Time To Listen

There are times when we simply do not have the time to stop what we are doing to listen to people who wish to talk with us about things that are important to them and may be important to us.

Usually when interrupted, we look up, sigh and say, "What is it?" or "Sit down, tell me what you have on your mind," but we are too distracted by other things to actually pay attention. We are too busy to listen, but we take a deep breath intending to try. About this time, the phone rings. We apologize, saying "Excuse me, I have to take this call," pick up, talk a while, distracted down another rabbit trail.

Now, neither of the three things on our plate actually has our full attention. The matter we were working on has been shoved aside, but still lingers as a distraction. The person we were about to talk with is sitting before us, and we're half-listening and trying to talk on the phone.

We've all been there. We put up walls, we shut doors, we say, "Absolutely no interruptions," but there is invariably some exception, often important. And, without listening, how can we tell whether it is or not?

Our natural human reaction to irksome interruptions or distractions is negative. We are
already halfway to saying "No" to a request, or
dismissing, out-of-hand, whatever the matter
concerns.

Bad listening or scheduling habits such as I
describe above probably account for a good
many bad decisions.

Until we have listened carefully to anything put
before us, we cannot make an intelligent, in-
formed decision.

Ninety percent of such interruptions may in
fact be a waste of our time; but, if we miss that
other 10 percent, we may do our clients a
disservice and our practices real damage over
time. If I'm listening while only partially focused, it's always plain to the person intruding
on my time. I think we all have to watch
ourselves here, because it becomes very easy to
slip into the habit of allowing intrusions, then
failing to do justice to ourselves or to those who
come to us.

There are times when you absolutely do not have time to devote to the problems people want to dump on your desk. Yet, these problems are important to the people who bring them to you. You should never sit there looking through the person to all the things beyond that you have on your mind.

An employee may be willing to accept a negative decision on a request; a client may be prepared to hear that his claim has no merit; a colleague may emphatically disagree with your suggestions. None of them, however, are prepared to deal with preoccupation. Moreover, you cannot honestly give any of these people a fair and considered answer unless you are prepared to listen to them.

The person coming to you may know his or her problem is not the biggest matter you have to handle, but there is no point in making him feel small or unimportant by literally looking through him while he is talking. The better way to handle ourselves at these times is to do the following:

• Tell the person, "I can't do this now, but

I will later, because I know it's important to you."

- Set a time when you can address the
  problem or listen.

- When you do so, focus on the problem;
  devote yourself entirely to the matter
  at hand.

The real point here is to be able to put each of
these willy-nilly distractions into a compart-
ment of time during which you will not try to
juggle five or more balls, but deal with one ball
at a time.

Over time, employees and associates will develop a sense of confidence from knowing that
you will give them a fair hearing, and fully
devote your attention to their problems *when
you have the time to do so.*

One way is to set specific time aside for anyone
and everyone's problems. Block that time off
consistently so everyone knows that you will
devote yourself to listening to and solving

problems during that period of time. This type of consistent and considerate scheduling will go a long way toward eliminating costly interruptions.

THERE ARE SOME THINGS THEY SHOULD HAVE DONE THEMSELVES

Bill Baker, a long-time friend and outstanding trial lawyer, explained that there was a time early in his career when employees and co-workers routinely abused his efforts at time management.

One day, out of frustration, he distributed a memo requiring anyone bringing a problem to him to put in writing the answer to the following four questions before bringing the problem to him:

1. What is the problem?
2. What is the cause of the problem?
3. What are all the possible solutions to the problem?
4. Which one do you suggest?

He told me he found this system in *How to Stop Worrying and Start Living* by Andrew Carnegie.

The system makes great sense. The employee is in the center of the loop, at the heart of the problem. To a large extent, she or he may be in a better position to analyze the problem and recommend a solution.

If it is a legal problem, obviously you are going to have to solve it, although an associate who comes up with such a problem and wants to discuss it should be able to answer the four questions above.

A client should be able to answer the first two questions and may know or have in mind possible solutions and suggest the one he or she would like to see effected—the state of the law and your ability to accomplish his desired goal permitting.

In this way, problems at worst come to you half-solved, or at least more fully known than before, and in the best cases do not come to you at all.

According to Bill, a great many relatively minor

problems had come to his desk in the past because he had not cultivated a sense of confidence in his employees and co-workers before he implemented his borrowed routine.

No One Ever Does Things As You Do Them

Lawyers, by nature, are highly critical thinkers. Sometimes we convince ourselves that we alone have the insight and fitness to be problem solvers around our office.

We recognize that if anyone in our office makes a serious mistake we too are responsible for that mistake. Therefore, our caution sometimes creates an unworkable system between attorney and staff.

One attorney explained her insights into this potential problem this way.

> I recognized years ago that perfection in all aspects of my practice was a great goal, but an impossibility in a real-life law office. Placing

my staff and co-workers under an unrealistic standard of perfection only resulted in the following:

- It placed me *de facto* in charge of everything no matter how in consequential the problem was.

- It stifled the creativity of my staff in that they were constantly apprehensive about taking action that might fall short of perfection.

- It had me reading, rereading, correcting, recorrecting, editing, and reediting even the most inconsequential pleadings, memos, and correspondence that passed from my staff to my desk.

We are all aware that there is no such thing as a successful pleading that "almost" states a cause of action or expert witness preparation that "almost" makes our expert appear credible. We recognize that there are some functions around our office that demand perfection, but we must also recognize that day-in-and-day-out total perfection is an unworkable standard for both ourselves and our staff. And herein lies the single most troubling aspect of leadership.

PEOPLE MAKE MISTAKES

The troublesome truth is that not everyone in our working or personal environments is as well trained or equipped as we are to avoid mistakes. The high side is that we also have a great deal of ability to rectify or fix things that do go wrong.

That does not excuse us for mistakes we make. It does, however, provide some consolation for what one leadership guru says is at the very heart of effective leadership and developing an organization that can operate without our keeping our hands on it at every moment. It is also how to develop a law practice we do not have to worry about while at lunch, or when in trial; one that can carry on, and do so effectively. The great principle is: *We have to let people make mistakes.*

When they do, we have to accept the consequences. It is one of the highest laws of leadership that when things go right, they get the credit; when things go wrong, we take the blame.

Living by that simple rule takes a huge amount of pressure off both us and our staff. You cannot do everything. You cannot be everywhere. You cannot be all things to all people, clients, and co-workers.

If a person who works for you or with you is afraid to make decisions, to take responsibility, and therefore wants you to ratify every decision or participate in reviewing and solving every problem that arises, you are in deep trouble.

I Wanted to Be a Lawyer, Not an Office Manager

One of the banes of law practice is that a lawyer has several hats to wear, one being that of leader around a law office that may be quite large and complex. For the most part, that job is not what we set out to do in life. We set out to practice law. We may have intended to be Atticus Finches or Roscoe Pounds, but within our domains, however large or small, we are becoming Lee Iacoccas.

Too bad organizational leadership was not part of our curriculum. It is, however, at the very heart of what we have to do to work effectively and manage our time so that we can have improved quality of life.

We've all seen the little sign: "Lead, follow, or get out of the way." If we don't assume leadership in our businesses, who will? No one. The corollary to this great truth is expressed by:

AN ORGANIZATION ALWAYS TAKES ON THE QUALITIES OF ITS LEADER

The above is an absolute rule. It is also a two-edged sword. If you are stressed-out and disorganized, so too, invariably, will be your supporting cast. If you are organized and focused, they just as invariably will mimic you.

If you are enthusiastic, diligent, organized, and helpful, the organization around you will take on those qualities. If you are tired, burned out, and irritable and have a pile of unfinished business all over your desk, you can be certain that, shortly, the rest of the office will be the same. It all flows from the top of any organization

There are any number of other equally effective ways to improve time or office management. If you are not successful in your efforts to manage time, I'd suggest you buy any of the many books on this subject and make it a point to read and follow the advice therein.

Advice is like medicine: Acquiring it does absolutely no good. Taking it does.

FAMILY OR PERSONAL TIME—
DOES ALL THIS STUFF WORK AT HOME?

The truth is many of the solutions we have discussed work at home. Certainly our personal lives will benefit from our utilizing them at work. The habit of organizing, sorting our priorities, and knowing (not vaguely, but specifically) what is important, worthwhile, effective, improve the quality of our lives.

You may have the impression that the *would do's* fall into the realm of our personal or family lives. Fact is, family and personal things are at least *should do's*; many are *must do's*.

By far the worst fear about our practices as trial lawyers is of "spending too much time practicing law and not enough time living." The second-highest expression of dissatisfaction with being a trial lawyer is, "The quality of life I have with my family suffers."

Around 40 percent "can't relax," or "have more of a negative outlook on life in general" than they had when they first started practicing law. Over half worry most about their practices while on vacation. Half fear burnout.

Somewhere on your working *must do* and *should do* list, you need to stop work in time to:

• Go home for dinner.

- Have lunch with a friend.
- Attend your daughter's piano recital or your son's football game.
- Run three (five, ten) miles.
- Read John Grisham's new best-selling novel.

You get the point.

For most of us, it is absolutely essential that in this juggling or balancing act of our lives, we learn to give higher priority to our personal and family lives.

We are creatures of habit who have adopted some very bad business and life management habits that have become too comfortable.

Chapter Eight

Achieving an Atticus-Like Quality of Life

Our search for Atticus Finch was motivated in large part because 76.2 per cent of us said: "I need to take more time from my day-to-day practice to improve my quality of life."

For most of us, being first in the office and last to leave each day does not provide much gratification in the quality-of-life arena. For some, however, being a slave to our practice is easier than fostering relationships or challenging our creativity or forcing ourselves to widen our horizons and grow intellectually.

We know how to be lawyers. We have become good at being lawyers. We have become task oriented with lawyering 60 hours a week in order to avoid the challenge of "living."

Living for most of us is not all the relaxation it is cracked up to be. For many of us, cross-examinations are easy, but the art of meaningfully interacting with our wives, children, and friends is an uncomfortable challenge. Focusing our creativity, intellect, and energy on our practice has become easier than saving part of ourselves for our health, hobbies, and spiritual growth.

Let's face it: improving the quality of our lives for ourselves is hard work if our natural instinct and ability to do so has begun to atrophy.

One lawyer made this observation about her practice:

> I practiced law for years without giving much thought to my "quality

of life." I began to figure out that, particularly in the practice of law, self-sacrifice is demanded and honored by our peers. We are honored more for our achievement and financial accomplishment than we are for our roles as wife, mother, and neighbor. We receive praise for denying ourselves a healthy balance between quality of life and professional demands.

Many of us are able to explain what a loss of quality of life means. We can adequately describe the tragedy of such a loss for our clients, but routinely ignore the loss in our own lives. Most of our best closing arguments probably were successful when we could adequately paint the picture of what a true loss of quality of life meant for our client. We probably explained to the jury that our client suffers because her quality of life suffers.

No doubt, we explained that our client's ability to live a full life is limited in that her personal relationships suffer, her ability to learn, to discover, and to participate in new hobbies is limited. We might have pointed out that our client seldom laughs or feels much joy because of her handicap. Much of what we might describe about our injured client's quality of life may sometimes look remarkably similar to our lives outside our function as a lawyer.

When we argue on behalf of our clients, we are explaining that in regard to quality of life, there is a division between the haves and the have-nots. I don't mean haves and have-nots in terms of economic class distinction, but haves and have-nots in terms of how we are permitted to enjoy life.

The past several decades of lawyering have created a chasm between the haves and the have-nots in the practice of law.

The haves are capable of huge self-sacrifices, but not at the expense of their family and friends. They recognize that self-sacrifice and quality of living must be balanced. Their self approval in how they reach that balance is of paramount importance. The have-nots convince themselves that self-sacrifice and quality living are mutually exclusive. They thrive on the praise they receive from the rest of the world and pay for it by deferring their quality living in exchange for their careers.

The haves are uncompromising in their unwillingness to accept a prototypical, preconceived method of practicing law from 9 a.m. to 9 p.m. for 35 years.

The have-nots require the safety and security of a noncreative, rote practice.

The haves believe in healthy competition—they are proud to win, but they do not let their need to win distort the way they live. The have-nots' infatuation with competition and winning creates a "me against them" attitude that touches even their most personal relationships and forces them to evaluate their happiness according to their win/loss ratio. They even judge their self-worth in a "me against them" fashion.

The haves figure out how to feel good about their level of professional and financial success as lawyers. The have-nots are so busy grabbing and acquiring wealth that they often forget what level of professional achievement they wanted to obtain, and in fact, they often cannot articulate what they want to buy or acquire in the process.

The haves recognize that the concept of "looking out for number one" is dated, cliche, and never very successful. The have-nots still believe that "looking out for number one" is a relevant way to live. They build their professional and private lives around this detached philosophy.

The haves believe that good quality of life is found in a series of small events that make day-to-day living enjoyable. They accept that their overall quality of life will rise or fall on tiny events such as time with the family, a new insight, an interesting conversation with a friend. The have-nots are always in search of the one huge special occurrence or event that is going to change their lives forever—the big case, the big project, the big break, the fireworks.

The haves are still children at heart. The have-nots have fastened every aspect of their lives to adulthood.

ALL OF US WERE CHILDREN ONCE— ATTICUS RETAINS WHAT WE HAVE LOST

While I cannot believe that any one of us who has searched has not found Atticus buried within, there is one key to how we should go about borrowing what Atticus knows.

If you have not already realized this central truth at the core of *To Kill A Mockingbird* and Atticus Finch, let me repeat what Harper Lee said of her own book in its epigram.

> *Lawyers, I suppose, were children once.*
> Charles Lamb

Pulitzer Prize–winning authors of books that ultimately become regarded as classics do not pluck such truths out of the ether.

What Harper Lee's choice of epigram tells us is that in both Atticus Finch and ourselves there is a child, in our case most likely lost or buried. Moreover, *To Kill A Mockingbird* shows that this lost or neglected aspect is surely the best part of us. It is quality of life embodied.

The child is discoverer, learner, seeker, believer, ever growing. The Atticus quality in each of us is manifested by a certain childlike honesty in the face of a sometimes dishonest world; it is unflagging integrity and devotion to principle when that principle is unpopular or unclear to others; it is a child's clear-eyed vision of what is good, fair and just, whether at work or play.

The fast lane of a law practice and of life sometimes has a tendency to make muddy and unclear things that should be easily recognizable. Unlike Atticus, our vision sometimes becomes blurred as we "mature," or become adults.

SEEING ATTICUS (AND OURSELVES) MAKES WHAT WAS MUDDY CLEARER

Some years ago, I was attending a seminar in New Orleans. I recall walking down Chartres

Street after dinner and looking in art gallery windows. In a small shop window a block or so below St. Louis Basilica, I saw a peculiar painting that disturbed me deeply. It was an oil on canvas of a Raggedy Ann doll nailed to a heavy beamed cross. The colors were dramatic, the imagery mean. The top of the cross leaned forward out of a dark and foreboding background. The doll's hair hung forward, covering part of a face whose traditional smile had been reversed. The flat cloth-doll fingerless hands were nailed through the palms with heavy steel spikes; the doll's legs were drawn together and nailed through the feet at the darker receding bottom of the painting. Suddenly, I realized that the candy-striped legs and feet I was seeing were not the flat stuffed legs and feet of a doll at all. They were the real legs of a little girl hidden in peppermint-striped leotards. Tacked to the easel beneath the painting was the epigram:

> *Adulthood draws nigh*
> *And we must gather up our toys*
> *Caress them one last time*
> *And put them away.*

"How true," I thought, suddenly believing I had understood exactly the painting's artistic or literary "truth." It seemed sad yet profound, but I realized that all of us have had to put away our toys, our childlike beliefs when we become adults, and sometimes we suffer in the process. Also inevitable and true, when we become adults and, eventually, in our own cases, professionals, the big trade-off that quite often seems not to have been totally worth the price is the one we made when we gave up all those childlike beliefs and "toys" for the mixed bag of blessings the life of a trial lawyer offers.

We assume responsibility for the affairs of others. We carry their their problems into the legal forum. We are paid to immerse ourselves in the role of advocate, counselor, and problem solver for individuals whose lives are typically upside-down with suffering and dissatisfaction; that huge responsibility solidifies our role as adults and it often saps our childlike spirit.

I believe the raggedy truth the artist was trying to convey was the same message taught by Harper Lee. That message is that we must be vigilant in not completely abandoning our child-like spirit.

When we abandon that spirit, we abandon the key to improving our quality of life. There is very little room for a childlike spirit within the armor we cover ourselves with as lawyers. Our armor makes us cynical. In my survey, 48.6 percent said they were much more suspicious of everyone since they began practicing law. Thirty-eight percent said, "I find I have a more negative outlook on life."

On the other hand, Atticus Finch—a decent man who saw the wisdom of not putting away his childhood—has not forgotten the skills and magic of childhood. He has no more forgotten who he is than "One-shot Finch" has forgotten how to shoot when he is called upon to kill a mad dog terrorizing the neighborhood.

ATTICUS UNDERSTANDS THE IMPORTANCE OF THE MOCKINGBIRD

Of all the admonitions he might have cast in concrete for Jem and Scout in giving them air-rifles, Atticus chooses only one:

> "I'd rather you shot at tin cans in the back yard, but I know you'll go after birds. Shoot all the blue jays you want, if you can hit 'em, but remember it's a sin to kill a mockingbird."

Scout says:

> That was the only time I ever heard Atticus say it was a sin to do something.

Miss Maudie tells Scout the reason. Mockingbirds (presumably unlike crows and jays) do no damage to crops, hurt no one nor anything. "Mockingbirds," she says, "don't do one thing but make music for us to enjoy" and "sing their hearts out for us."

There are perhaps as many ways to interpret what the "mockingbird" in *To Kill A Mockingbird* means as there are meanings to ponder about Herman Melville's great white whale in *Moby Dick*.

The mockingbird can mean something as simple and trite as "stop and smell the flowers." It can be a metaphor for the tragic death of Tom Robinson, who never did anything wrong, but rather offered help to one who needed it.

But above all, I believe, the mockingbird represents the pure heart and joy found in the unending song of childhood, a song certain people continue to sing in the face of all the world's travails ... a song many in our profession appear to have forgotten.

When, in the press of lawyering, some of us lose our enthusiasm, our belief in ourselves and others, what happens is that we lose our childlike faith that life can be all we once believed in. Atticus shows that a person can retain, or in our case, regain that faith by living and teaching the lessons of childhood.

Harper Lee constantly illustrates throughout her book how the journey toward adulthood forces us to give up our childlike ways, sometimes to our credit and sometimes to our detriment.

For example, Atticus believes that his son, Jem, is tormenting Boo Radley when in fact, Boo appreciates Jem's child's play, so Atticus sets out to catch Jem in the act of "tormenting" Boo. Atticus pretends to leave the house for work then comes back and catches Jem trying to send a message by holding it up to Boo's room on the tip of a fishing pole.

Atticus expresses his disappointment to Jem and explains that Jem needs to be more conscious of his conduct. Atticus asks Jem: "You want to be a lawyer, don't you?" Jem waits until Atticus walks away out of hearing distance and shouts:

> "I thought I wanted to be a lawyer,
> but I ain't so sure now."

Jem's real fear is that when he becomes a lawyer, an adult, he will have lost the most precious thing he has, the thing we see him slowly losing throughout the book—his innocence, his childhood, his suspension of disbelief. In the end, Jem realizes, as most of us should by now, that unlike most adults, Atticus has both his childhood and something more—a full and rich life as both a lawyer and a person.

There is no doubt in my mind that each of us who will search for Atticus will find him in the child buried in ourselves. That child is recoverable if we want to dig and work at becoming more open, more childlike in seeking out and experiencing a new and more meaningful life and law practice.

We will never be children again, but if we work at it, we can regain the same childlike enthusiasm for our lives that Atticus demonstrates. One of the oldest lessons of the Judaeo-Christian tradition is that one has only to see with (or through) the eyes of a child for it to be clear what is good, best, right—what quality is and what it is not.

HOW SHALL WE PURSUE THE ATTICUS-LIKE QUALITY OF LIFE SO MANY OF US DESIRE?

The majority of us have a belief that lawyering takes a heavy toll on our overall quality of life.

If you asked ten attorneys what factors they consider important in evaluating quality of life, the following list would be points of discussion:

- The quality of their health, both physical and emotional.

- The quality of their relationships with their immediate families.

- The quality of their relationships with friends.

- The quality of their living environment.

- The quality and frequency of their leisure activity.

- Their level of satisfaction or dissatisfaction with their work and working environment.

- Their level of satisfaction or dissatisfaction with intellectual and creative challenges, both inside and outside their practices;

- Their financial comfort.

- The quality of their spiritual growth—an understanding that it is not enough simply to nurture one's body, but just as necessary to nurture one's spirit.

I am not skilled enough in the practice of life or lawyering to provide specific advice that will solve all possible problems falling into the categories above. I am a lawyer, not a guru, psychologist, or psychoanalyst. I am merely the tour director of an expedition that set out to find Atticus Finch in ourselves.

Most of us have made a good living by focusing our intellect and energy toward the process of solving problems for other people. We deserve no less for ourselves. We are well equipped to recognize and define our problems and seek out and implement solutions to basic traps that keep us from succeeding fully as human beings. We are limited only by cynicism and the arrogance of believing that there are no problem solvers more adept than ourselves.

Most of us seek better-quality living in an "OJT" approach. We hope we will learn as we go. We seek a better quality of life with blinders on our eyes. Those blinders cause us to miss and ignore the wealth of creative thought abundant in self-help books and motivational books that have been with us for centuries. Many of us have convinced ourselves that we are too smart for and don't need centuries of valuable insights into living.

Again, a huge percentage of questionnaire respondents said they have never read a motivational book.

BEING FULFILLED IS "QUALITY OF LIFE" ATTICUS'S LIFE IS A FULFILLING ONE

As we have moved through this search together, we have discussed many specific steps we can take to adjust our law practices to allow us time and energy to expand other facets of our lives.

We are not seeking lives without problems. A life without problems or challenges would be dull. What we do want is to get off old, redundant, tiresome, energy-sapping problems and move forward toward new and more energy-producing struggles.

We are climbing a new mountain, not plowing the same old fields, tilling tired old soil in the valley. The goal should be to revitalize our lives if we feel we need it.

REFINING AND RENEGOTIATING OLD CONTRACTS

The difficulty we face in revitalizing our lives is this: In each facet of our lives, we have undertaken obligations, we have made promises, and we have projected, however vaguely, certain futures both for ourselves and for others. In fulfilling these obligations or contracts, we have become either fulfilled or dissatisfied.

We seem to have less trouble fulfilling our lawyer's employment contract with clients and our law partners than we have with honestly and generously fulfilling those many unwritten contracts we have made with our spouses, families, friends, neighbors, and ourselves.

One measure of the success of our lives is how we keep the promises we have implicitly and explicitly made – how we honor our contracts. An even greater measure of what quality of life we are to enjoy is in how we keep, honor, and fulfill the unwritten promises in our own lives. I believe there is a necessity to recognize and fulfill our obligations and contracts with ourselves and those outside our legal world with the same diligence and devotion with which we fulfill those written obligations within our role as lawyers.

Rather than default on our contracts within our own lives, we now must conscientiously renegotiate, and honor, those contracts. In doing so, we will find ourselves achieving a higher quality of life. Our lives are so intertwined with the lives of others that this process of renegotiatiation requires that we include all significant parties.

WITH SPOUSE OR SIGNIFICANT OTHER

There are exceptions that have been created by the modern world—prenuptial or live-in agreements being the most common—but most of us entered our more intimate relationships in a more casual and loving way. Motivated by the heart, we asked someone else to share our lives.

We made promises. Some may have been explicit: "When I have built my law practice to a 10-attorney firm, I will be able to spend more time with the family." Some were implied in the marriage ceremony. We promised to be one with each other "for richer or poorer, in sickness and in health," and so on. It was through thick and thin, boom times or lean, bull or bear markets, etc. We pledged ourselves to be members of a team. We have made promises that touch on all facets of our joint lives—personal, social, and financial—with that team member.

One of the clearest and most essential rules of leadership is that one never marches off into battle without one's troops motivated and trained to undertake the mission and accomplish it. Focused cooperation is the essential element of any type of team work.

Whatever we contemplate by way of adjusting or redistributing our private or family time, we cannot succeed without some reassessment of our obligations to people who share our lives.

You can imagine the howl you would certainly create this evening if you were to rush through the door of your home and initiate the following dialogue:

> "Honey, it's me, I'm home! I have this great idea: We really have far too much stuff; our lives are not as rich as they should be; we don't have as much family time together as we should; so I've decided to take care of all that."

> *"That's great, and you know I'm glad you're home early, but I've got to pick up the kids at school. Can we talk about this later?"*

> "No, sweetheart, we have to get cracking. I've decided to be more like Atticus Finch."

"Who?"

"You know, the wonderful lawyer, father, family man, good neighbor, and noble character from *To Kill A Mockingbird.* Life is easier and more rewarding for him because he has a general practice in a small town, everything goes along slower there... the pace of our lives will be different. I'll walk to work and back – maybe even come home for lunch. I'll have much, much more time for you and the kids."

"Really? What's the problem, honey? Bad day in court? Listen, I have always told you that you work too hard, but . . . the Atticus Finch I remember lived in a five-room house, light-years from civilization . . . how will we live?"

"No problem. We can live a long time off the money we get from selling everything. . . . We'll get by."

You get the picture. Any one of us can imagine our own scenario here in the light of what kind of relationships we have agreed to. Whatever our situation, we do have agreements with our spouses.

The same principles apply to our children. Imagine that you call a conclave of your children and announce that in the middle of high school, or wherever they are, "We're all moving to Maycomb."

Or how about this:

> "Son, I know we haven't spent as much time together as we should, so I'm now going to make all that change. From now on, I'm going with you everywhere—we're going to spend every weekend fishing together. I'm even going to teach you to make fishing lures. We'll start a father-son bowling league."

Or, tell your daughter who doesn't see you for a week at a time when you are in trial:

"Honey, we just have to do more things together, so I've arranged for us to take Modern Dance three evenings a week, and I'd like to hang out at the mall with you and your friends on weekends."

These people, our children, have lives, friends, and hierarchies of their own. In our frequent absences and in spite of our tardiness for events of importance, they have developed friends and routines. They have settled into their lives with or without our participation.

If we want to spend more time—quality time—making our relationships richer, then probably all we really need to do is repair a few cracks in the walls of our lives, not bring the building down. We do not need to be Atticus Finch to borrow his best qualities. We certainly do not need to live in Maycomb to do so.

Our goal is not to become poor and live in Depression-era Maycomb. It is to become successful both as lawyers and human beings; we might even say we have embarked on a program to acquire "fatter souls." We are obligated to discuss such goals with those who might be affected. They too will benefit from the process.

With Law Partners and Associates

Most of the changes we might choose to make in our ability to deal with overworking and underliving will be of direct benefit to anyone with whom we practice law. The firm is going to have a far more enthusiastic and efficient lawyer in its ranks. It is just not going to have him around quite as much or so much at the beck and call of anyone with an itch to scratch.

In thinking of Southern literature, as *To Kill A Mockingbird* makes one do, I recalled a great story about William Faulkner. Early in his career, he needed a job to support himself while writing, so he got appointed postmaster of Oxford, Mississippi. After a while, people started complaining about not getting their mail. An investigation showed Faulkner was busy writing and just did not have time to put up all the mail. He had been throwing it out in the trash.

Confronted, he is reputed to have said, "I can't be at the beck and call of every sonofabitch with a three-cent stamp."

Atticus Finch somehow makes time for everything and everyone who is important in his life, or, just as essential, in whose life he is important. But remember: each of us, too, has a creative life that cannot or should not be at the beck and call of anyone with a quarter to put in a phone or anyone who happens to share an office with us.

In seeking a change in our obligations to law partners, we have to be open and fair but firm in making those adjustments that will enable us to live a full life as a person and as a lawyer. After all, a law partnership is nothing less than a professional marriage. In addition, we may have obligations to associates as well. If we have undertaken to bring them along, to lead and supervise their growth from associate to partner, we owe them the same duties within the professional marriage as we owe our children in our private lives. We can be faithful to partners and associates and at the same time be faithful to ourselves and whatever new vision becoming more Atticus-like mandates.

These changes may require more creativity on your part. Lawyers all over the country are being creative in attempting to improve their quality of life by making adjustments in their commitments to their partners.

Try it yourself.

For example, schedule two or even three days per week where your work schedule permits you to go into the office at 3:00 p.m. or 4:00 p.m. and work until 10:00 p.m. or 11:00 p.m. You will be able to work uninterrupted on such things as pleadings, correspondence, and trial strategy planning in an environment that you have complete control over.

If your goal is to improve your quality of life by allowing yourself time to "live" during your regular working week, then this type of "alternative scheduling" should help dramatically. Such alternative scheduling only requires commitment to the goal of improving your quality of living.

If such alternative scheduling is simply too radical for the way you view your world, at least consider maintaining the same work schedule that you presently have, but carry out your work in a setting outside your office for two to three days per week. That change of setting for many attorneys involves working at home, at the beach house, on their sailboat docked at a pier, at a hunting camp, at a ski cabin, or even at the public library.

Attorneys who are willing to make such adjustments recognize that taking advantage of portable phones and fax machines to gain better control over their work environment is a simple, small step towards improving their quality of life.

The difficulty with such thinking for most attorneys is that they feel that they have already arrived at the "best way" to be a lawyer. In almost every aspect of our law practice, it is risky to assume that the way we are doing things is the "best way." Indeed, the work environments most of us participate in are practical but far from the "best way" to practice law and maintain a good quality of life.

There is great danger in concluding that we must work from 7:00 a.m. to 7:00 p.m. or that we must accept all the trappings of the prototype work environment that have evolved and been handed down to us from decades of lawyering.

I mentioned earlier that the ABA survey shows that the vast majority of lawyers do not take all the vacation time allotted to them. They give it back to their practices, their firms. If our adjustments in stress reduction and time management are effective, we should be capable of—and absolutely must insist on—utilizing this important renewal tool.

The sabbatical is another important kind of revitalization program. It is becoming more and more common in larger law firms and even finding favor with small firms or single practitioners.

We have inklings in *To Kill A Mockingbird* that Atticus's sabbatical from everyday life and law practice is in his retreats to Montgomery when he serves in the legislature or when he and the family go to visit Aunt Alexandra at Finch's Landing.

In a recent article by Gregory Eisland in *Trial* under "The Complete Lawyer" and "Sabbaticals," he discusses the resistance some firms have to such programs and some of the worries lawyers have about taking them.

Many attorneys have a reluctance to "rewrite" or "renegotiate" the relationship they have with the rest of their partners because they are fearful that in their absence someone will have to take up their load.

GETTING A LIFE

Among fears lawyers have when considering a sabbatical are financial worries such as "How can I afford to leave my workload unattended and not earn what I normally project?" or, in a prolonged absence, "Will my clients jump ship?"

Some lawyers indicate they even fear being without the pressures of practicing law. It is as if they cannot imagine a life without pressures and deadlines driving them to burnout. To them, Eisland says,

> Get a life. I love practicing law, too, but there are other dimensions to existence. Simply practicing law is not enough. You need some time when you can take a longer view—relax awhile—forget your law degree—stop analyzing everything—just lean back and enjoy.

In order to apply the advice given by Mr. Eisland, you must first be partners with attorneys whose horizons are high enough and sophisticated enough to understand the importance of "living." Fortunately, you have complete control over that problem in that you alone choose your partners. John Merting, a single practitioner, explained that life is simply too short to be giving up too much of it to business partners:

> Making time to live for yourself and your family takes the same

caliber of commitment that you devote to your clients. Sometimes, it is hard work finding time to live outside your world of lawyering. I have represented dozens of clients who have no quality of life through no choice of their own. I do have a choice, and there is one thing I'm pretty sure of – This ain't no dress rehearsal; it is now or never.

Nickolas Geeker, a trial judge, made this observation about trial lawyers:

My life and the lives of my family members are important enough to me that I demanded time for all of us to "live" as a family. I see trial lawyers before me every day who have diminished their quality of life in search of fame and fortune. I doubt that, on their death bed, they will say "I wish I had handled one more big case." Instead, it is more likely that they will say, "I wish I had traveled more, learned more, lived more."

Charles Gibson of Jackson, Mississippi, explained it this way:

> We are driven away from balance and improved quality of life because most of us are constantly in the "state of becoming." We are seldom content with the place we occupy and we have programmed ourselves to press on to "become more."

There is nothing wrong with the process of "becoming" as Charles Gibson describes it, unless "becoming" has actually turned into a process of merely "acquiring."

WE BECOME WHAT WE THINK ABOUT

Single-mindedly acquiring recognition, status, position, and wealth alone as lawyers inevitably results in a deplorable quality of life. It is a quality of life that is completely self-imposed. If there is any truth to the concept that we become what we think about and visualize in our lives, then there does exist opportunity for change.

When Dorothy was in Oz and wanted to go home, she could attain only what she could visualize. Once she could visualize friends, family, and the comfort of her home, she was halfway there.

Most of us became lawyers in part because that is what we spent years of our lives thinking about and visualizing. Now that we are lawyers it seems appropriate to consider what we are "thinking about" as to how we want to live our lives as lawyers. We can visualize ourselves as overstretched, hurry sick, professional successes, or we can constantly, vigilantly think about being successful professionals with balance in our lives. Either way, it is a truth that we become what we think about.

In one of his lectures, Lord Acton (John E. E. Dalbery-Acton) suggested that a person should, "Learn as much by writing as reading." I think that has happened for me. In trying to read the road map for us all, a great deal of what I once failed to understand about lawyering has become clearer.

I began in Chapter One by stating:

> The question I wanted to ask, and, honestly answer, was: *Inasmuch as I started out to be a lawyer much like Atticus, have I succeeded?*

> My answer was, "Only partially," which led to the next question: "Why not fully?"

I'd like to revisit that question and perhaps the answers it leads to here.

There was a time in life when I thought the most important thing I could do for myself was to live life in such a way as to minimize the cynicism I saw around me and sometimes felt myself, a life where I didn't let anger and frustration creep into so many things that bothered me.

One of my goals was to reach a point where I felt peaceful, maybe even serene about who I am and what I was doing. Moreover, I hoped always to feel a real appreciation for what I had, without worrying about what I didn't have.

The point is, I thought lawyering could help me do that, that lawyering would give me control over the things that made me cynical, angry or frustrated. I envisioned that once I became a lawyer I would have a job where I had this control. Many of you have expressed similar goals or early hopes.

Yet, in writing this book and examining our common lives as lawyers, it has become apparent that whatever control over our lives we sought by becoming lawyers we have lost in the way we now live as lawyers.

Perhaps most of us forgot what we were after. Perhaps we stopped visualizing and thinking about *how* we were going to gain control of our lives by lawyering. It is possible that many of us no longer visualize ourselves growing or evolving in our lives. At the bottom line, "quality of life" depends on living both a rich professional life and a meaningful and rewarding private one.

To Grow We Must Think about Growing

In all times and in all places in human history, a certain well-rounded excellence of character and behavior, a certain quality-manifestation of intellect, emotion, and physical hardiness have been universally admired wherever they appeared.

There are many examples of those with physical handicaps or disabilities achieving balance and acclaim. There are few examples of those with intellectual, emotional, or ethical deficits to be found on this honor roll.

Whether there is some universal or higher law that governs this process is a question for theologians, philosophers, or individuals to judge in their own hearts. Regardless of its origin, this overall excellence in human conduct and purpose has been prized and praised in all times and all places.

Seeking this specific excellence has been one road to arriving at an improved quality of life. The Greeks called this excellence "arete," which at times has been translated as "virtue." However, most scholars agree that *arete* was more than mere virtue in the original context. It meant something more akin to an absolute devotion to duty—not duty to others, but one's duty to oneself, a striving for excellence in *all* things. *Arete* is a personal, not a public example. It is an inner standard. The fact that its aura is plain for all with eyes to see does not make it an external quality. Put simply, the Greek warrior sought excellence as a poet, artist, musician, scholar, teacher, and soldier. Likewise, Atticus understands that there is no "virtue" in his role as a lawyer alone.

What the Greeks called *arete,* the Japanese called "Bushido." This *Bushido* code of the Japanese warrior also called for excellence in all things, military, familial, and artistic. *Bushido*—"the way of the warrior"—comes from the Chinese word for warrior, knight, or man of arms. It was the code of the Japanese warrior that stressed self-improvement, bravery, and full but simple living.

The reward for living the code of *Bushido* was

not found in public accolades and acceptance, but in self-acceptance and self-approval. In living the code of *Bushido*, it was believed that quality of the spirit was improved through growth.

In all examples where the highest kinds of excellence have been sought, by all assortments of cultures, *balance* between and among the physical, mental, and emotional life is the major focus. Such a balance is rarely ever achieved or sustained by most of us; however, we improve our quality of life in the process of constantly, vigilantly striving for that balance. The effort can be as rewarding as the end result.

The simplicity of such concepts of *arete* or *Bushido* is that by merely doing the best we can with what we have, we move toward excellence, and in the process an improved quality of life falls into place. *Achieving* excellence is unimportant except for the most compulsive/retentive personality. It is the journey toward excellence that improves our quality of living. That journey of "becoming" is more rewarding than a journey of acquiring.

This concept is ageless. It can be rearranged, restated, retitled, but it can never be distorted. We should pay attention.

Atticus learned and lived the way of *Bushido* and *arete* out of instinct. No instruction was necessary because the concepts are so universally understood by people who are watching and listening.

More important, it does not appear that Atticus sought or expected much recognition for the way he lived his life. But his lack of expectation was rewarded.

If we live our lives with the overall excellence of *arete* and *Bushido*, we will have the higher quality of life we set out to acquire in our *Search for Atticus Finch*.

Will this cause our light as lawyers to shine any brighter among our fellow citizens? And even if it would, should that be the reason for our doing so? The answer to the first question is yes, others are going to see us in a different light.

The answer to the second question is no. We are doing this for ourselves just as Atticus lives his highest and best life for himself. Still, if we do so, our lack of expectation will be rewarded just as his was.

Every person or thing Atticus touches is made better for his passing. We all "stand up" when an Atticus-like excellence, in whatever form, passes. We may not do so physically, may not take off our hats, but we are uplifted.

If Atticus has taught us nothing else, we know we stand taller when we serve, when we reach down to help others rise rather than try to stand on their necks or backs in order to be bigger.

We don't have to go to Japan or understand ancient Greek philosophy to see and understand these principles. We see them in everything we know.

When the great architect Christopher Wren was buried in London's magnificently domed St. Paul's cathedral, the spires of more than a hundred lesser churches he had designed could be seen across London. The epitaph chosen for Wren's tomb was:

HERE LIES
CHRISTOPHER WREN
READER, IF YOU SEEK A MONUMENT
LOOK AROUND YOU.

Harper Lee closes *To Kill A Mockingbird* with Atticus tucking Scout into bed, and Scout saying of Arthur "Boo" Radley, who had finally come out, "Atticus, he was real nice." And Atticus replying, "Most people are, Scout, when you finally see them."

We have seen Atticus Finch and the monument that he has left behind in Harper Lee's classic recollection of him. The question for each of us to answer, and act upon, is this: When we have passed through our lives, what is a "reader" of our legacy to see when asked to "look around?"

Understanding Atticus Finch illustrates the proof that each of us can write or rewrite our own lives. If we do so, when we have passed perhaps those looking around and recalling who we were will be able to take off their hats when they read in stone:

HERE LIES
[YOUR NAME]
A TRIAL LAWYER
WHO, LIKE ATTICUS FINCH,
SERVED HONORABLY
IN LAW AND LIFE.

APPENDIX

(THE SURVEY)

List the most significant fears you have about your practice as a trial lawyer:

64.1%	Fear of spending too much time practicing law and not enough time living
58.2%	Fear that the practice of law as a plaintiff's trial lawyer is being threatened by political and social changes beyond my control
53.4%	Fear of not generating enough business
53.4%	Fear of failing in trial
49.9%	Fear of burnout
41.5%	Fear of dissatisfied clients
30.8%	Fear of being sued
17.8%	Fear of ethics complaints
10.7%	Fear of never having enough recognition as a trial lawyer among my peers
10.7%	Fear of being a failure in my profession
4.7%	Fear of the courtroom setting
4.7%	Fear of judges

List the top events in your practice as a plaintiff's trial lawyer that cause you the most dissatisfaction with your job:

57.5%	I have become less of a legal scholar and more of a businessman
56.3%	The quality of life I have with my family suffers
42.5%	Some of my fears about my job as a trial lawyer cause me dissatisfaction
40.0%	My emphasis on making money detracts from my creative, inventive ability as a lawyer
33.0%	I have always wanted to forge new fields and concepts in the practice of law, but I don't have time
31.3%	The public image of plaintiff's trial lawyers affects my self image
21.3%	My day-to-day routine is too similar or repetitive
16.3%	I don't get enough recognition among my partners and peers for my abilities as a lawyer

I worry most about my practice when:

65.8%	I am at work
62.1%	In the middle of the night when I should be sleeping
44 7%	While I am on vacation
27.3%	I seldom worry about my practice

I need to take more time from my day to day practice to:

76.2%	Improve my quality of life
55.1%	Participate in organizations that are involved with improving such things as the

> welfare of children, the welfare of the
> elderly, etc.

50.4%   Market myself better
36.7%   Learn a new hobby
32.8%   Write articles in professional journals
31.7%   Participate in political groups that further
        the best interests of trial lawyers
17.6%   Handle pro bono cases

I read motivational books:

43.8%   Never read them
19.1%   I read one last year
14.6%   I don't need them
13.3%   At least once a week
 8.9%   Only when I his rock bottom

I have read at least one book about how to deal with stress:

59.6%   No
40.4%   Yes

Since the time I graduated from law school, I have enrolled in nonlegal educational courses in local colleges:

80.9%   Never
11.9%   More than twice
 2.4%   More than five times

The following would be correct about the way I approach work:

72.2%   I am most productive in short spurts
        throughout the day
69.8%   I am good about returning telephones calls
68.6%   I do things in an order of importance
59.2%   I dictate answers to mail within three days

of the time I receive it

35.5%	I put tough decisions off as long as possible
32.0%	I am a good organizer
30.7%	I am a good delegator
22.5%	My desk is generally well organized
5.9%	I delegate too much
3.6%	I am fearful of returning calls because of what my client might say

We should begin limiting the number of new law schools and new law school graduates

58%	Yes
42%	No

Some older, successful, trial lawyers have caused much harm to the image of trial lawyers through the excessively boastful image they have portrayed to the general public:

44.8%	Yes
24.1%	No
31.0%	The good they have done outweighs whatever harm they might have caused

The following best describes my attitudes during trial:

72.4%	Cross examinations are stressful but enjoyable most of the time
57.7%	If it is a dead heat up to closing arguments, my chances of pulling it out during closing are good
52.8%	I enjoy *voir dire*
51.5%	Most of the time I have an accurate gut feeling by closing argument as to what will happen
39.3%	I have tried cases against attorneys whom

	I thought were truly better trial lawyers than me on more than three occasions
35.6%	Opening statement and direct examinations are the most comfortable parts of the trial for me whether I am winning or losing
26.9%	*Voir dire* causes me great anxiety because I am concerned about loose cannons in the crowd
24.5%	I sometimes find myself playing it too safe during trial because I am fearful of what the judge's reaction might be if I do otherwise
15.9%	I think the idea that I learn more from my losses than my wins is ridiculous
14.7%	When I lose at trial I sometimes feel that the jury did not like me personally
11.0%	Winning at trial is more a function of your luck in picking a jury than it is your skill in presentation
6.1%	I don't like to cross-examine

Which of the following do you notice about yourself now, that you did not notice when you first began practicing as a trial lawyer?

48.6%	I am much more suspicious of everyone
42.4%	I have become more motivated
41.1%	I can't relax
38.6%	I find I have more of a negative outlook on life in general
33.6%	I am more conscious of the way I am perceived by my peers
32.4%	I become bored more easily
28.7%	I find myself constantly dissatisfied with my level of success in life
28.7%	I always want more
19.9%	I am less considerate of my friends and family
18.7%	I am unhappy more than I am happy

17.4%   I have never been happier
17.4%   I am less ambitious
17.4%   I have become more creative and well
        rounded in my personal life
14.9%   I have become more optimistic in general

I am, in my opinion, a Type A personality:

68.2%   Yes
31.8%   No

I discuss career alternatives with my closest friends:

48.3%   Seldom
31.5%   Never
20.2%   Often

I have set a target for the age at which I will:

57.4%   I have no specific well-defined long-term goals
18.4%   Retire from the practice totally
10.3%   Write my first book
 5.7%   Stop trying cases
 8.0%   Make a career change

I am a trial lawyer because:

64.8%   I like the excitement and fast pace
54.0%   This is what my personality is best suited for
51.6%   I enjoy conflict when I am on the right side
48.0%   I have or will have made a meaningful
        impact to better society as a whole by the
        time I leave my practice as a trial lawyer
34.8%   It is a purely financial decision
24.0%   I am afraid to make a career change at this
        point in my life

22.8%   I like the recognition I get within my community as a trial lawyer

The following best describes my work schedule:

53.5%   8:00 a.m. to 6:00 p.m. Monday through Friday and part day Saturday and Sunday

20.9%   8:30 a.m. to 5:00 p.m. Monday through Friday and part day Saturday

16.3%   I vary my schedule; often I take off during the day and work 5:00 p.m. till 10:00 p.m.; otherwise my schedule is basically 8:00 a.m. to 5:00 p.m. Monday through Friday

19.3%   8:00 a.m. to 5:00 p.m. most days, but typically I take 1/2 day off between Monday and Friday

The following best describes the way I approach my job day to day:

51.1%   I have no specific time set aside to perform particular tasks day to day

33.3%   I let my secretary do my scheduling for appointments; depositions, etc., and then I perform repetitive daily tasks as best I can around that scheduling throughout the day

1.1%   I set a specific time for performing particular tasks such as returning all my calls; completing all my dictation; talking to adjusters, etc.

I find the level of stress I experience as a trial lawyer is:

42.5%   More than moderate
37.1%   Moderate
15.7%   Extreme
4.5%   Mild

Within the last year I have made written responses to newspapers or other media that have engaged in what I consider to be "lawyer bashing":

46.7%	Never
36.0%	Once
12.0%	Twice
2.7%	Three times
2.7%	More than three times

I have been practicing actively as a trial lawyer for:

45.6%	More than 15 years
32.9%	More than 5 years
21.5%	More than 10 years

I am a board-certified civil trial lawyer:

13.1%	Yes
86.9%	No

In a typical year, I will try:

41.3%	More than 3 cases
35.0%	More than 5 cases
23.8%	More than 10 cases

I have perceived my job as a trial lawyer becoming more difficult within

31.8%	The last 3 years
29.5%	The last 5 years
26.1%	I don't perceive any difference from when I first began practicing
12.5%	The last year